ROMANS

A commentary on chapters 1 – 8

ROMANS

A commentary on chapters 1 – 8

by
ALBERT LECKIE

PRECIOUS SEED PUBLICATIONS

First published September 2007

ISBN 978-1-871642-22-3

Printed in China

Contents

PREFACE

A few words regarding the fact that this book is being published nearly twenty years after Albert Leckie was called home to be with the Lord might help the reader to appreciate its contents and format.

For nearly thirty years Mr. Leckie conducted the Trimsaran Bible Readings in south west Wales. These were held in August each year and proved to be helpful to many believers in their understanding of a wide range of truth. The years 1981-84 were devoted to the study of the first ten chapters of the Roman epistle. These Readings were unlike many others. It is usual in Bible Readings for there to be a set passage and in the time available this must be covered, with the result that some verses are not considered in any depth or at all. At Trimsaran there was no set passage: the meeting continued until the arrival of the time for it to finish and the next day the study began at the next verse. This ensured a more even coverage of each verse and meant that the text could be considered in greater detail.

Tape recordings of the Trimsaran Bible Readings have become available within the last few years. These have been transcribed and edited into a form suitable for publication and this book is the result. A few verses in chapter 8 were not covered on these tapes and material from ministry given by our brother has been inserted. Strenuous efforts have been made to discover the whereabouts of our brother's notes on Romans (and many other of his notes, particularly those bound in Oxford Loose Leaf Bible covers) but they have not been successful. A plea is made that if their whereabouts are known they be made available to assist in future publications.

Because of the way the book has been prepared it has not been possible to include any bibliography or references. It is unlikely that everything in this book is original but the reader will discover delightful lines of truth not commonly expressed elsewhere.

The publishers are grateful to Mrs. Grace Browne of Bath for proof reading the manuscript and for the wholehearted encouragement of Mr. Leckie's sister, Mrs. Winnie Lee, of Carluke, Lanarkshire, in this work.

May the Lord be pleased to use these notes on Romans to the blessing of the Lord's people, that there might be a deeper understanding of the gospel we love and a greater desire to communicate it to others, even as the apostle to the Gentiles desired to do at Rome.

Ian Jackson
Eastbourne
June, 2007

THE EPISTLE TO THE ROMANS

BACKGROUND AND OUTLINE

Author   There is no doubt that the apostle Paul was the author. See chapter 1 verse 1.

Time of writing   Paul had not visited Rome at the time of writing the epistle. As the apostle of the uncircumcision, Rome was within the sphere of his labour. In chapter 15 verse 16 he describes himself as 'the minister of Jesus Christ to the Gentiles' and in Galatians chapter 2 verse 7 he states that 'the gospel of the uncircumcision was committed unto me'. There is one gospel for both Jews and Gentiles but Paul had special responsibility with regard to the Gentiles. James, Cephas and John gave him 'the right hands of fellowship' for him to 'go unto the heathen', Gal. 2. 9. Rome was therefore in the sphere of Paul's labour.

Paul had desired to go to Rome for a long time. In chapter 15 verse 23 he refers to his 'great desire these many years to come unto you'. See also Acts chapter 19 verse 21 where Paul says, 'I must also see Rome'. He fully intended to visit there and did so in unexpected circumstances; not as a preacher, but as a prisoner, three years after this epistle was penned. He was there in a hired lodging, Acts 28. 30, and from there he wrote the prison epistles. It is clear from chapter 16 that he knew many saints there.

Place of writing   If the Gaius of 1 Corinthians chapter 1 verse 14 is the same person as the Gaius of chapter 16 verse 23, 'Gaius mine host', this epistle was written at Corinth. 'Erastus the chamberlain' is referred to also in chapter 16 verse 23 and he appears to have belonged to Corinth, 2 Tim. 4. 20. Additionally, in chapter 16 verse 1, Paul commends Phoebe who came from Cenchrea, a place near to Corinth.

Time of writing   Paul wrote the epistle after fully preaching in the Adriatic area and when he was about to leave Greece with gifts for the poor at Jerusalem, cf. 15. 19, 25.

To whom written   In chapter 1 verse 7 the letter is addressed 'To all that be in Rome'. It is important to remember that the majority were Gentiles. In chapter 1 verse 6, he spoke of the nations 'among whom are ye also the called of Jesus Christ' and, in chapter 1 verse 13, he expressed his desire to have fruit among them, 'even as among other Gentiles'. There were also Jews who were converts from the day of Pentecost. Acts chapter 2 verse 10 refers to 'strangers of Rome, Jews and proselytes'.

There is no record of the church at Rome being planted by an apostle. There is divine wisdom here because of the later, pretentious claims of the Roman Catholic church in connection with Peter and apostolic succession.

Paul gave the saints at Rome a great commendation in indicating that he considered them to be spiritually mature, 15. 14. Priscilla and Aquila were resident there, 16. 3, and Andronicus and Junia were of note among the apostles, 16. 7. We also learn from Philippians chapter 1 verse 14 that there were those in Rome who were bold to preach the gospel.

The epistle was actually written by Tertius, 16. 22, and was conveyed to Rome by Phoebe, a sister visiting Rome on business. One cannot help but contrast this to all the pomp of the Roman Catholic church.

Subject   The Gospel of God is the great subject of the book, 1. 1. 'A just God and a Saviour', Isa. 45. 21, could be written over this epistle. In Exodus chapter 34 verse 7, God declared Himself, One who 'will by no means clear the guilty'. Proverbs chapter 17 verse 15 states that to justify the wicked is an abomination, yet in chapter 3 verse 26 the apostle states that God is 'just, and the justifier of him which believeth in Jesus'. A just God can now clear the guilty who believe.

Romans has been termed the greatest book of logic in the world. Its logic is that every conceivable argument against the gospel is taken up and dismissed by the apostle.

The teaching of the epistle is so very relevant today. There are three things in which saints today are becoming remiss, namely: the doctrine of the gospel; dispensational truth; and practical Christianity. All of these are matters dealt with in this book, which may be broadly divided in the following way.

CHAPTERS 1-8 DOCTRINAL

The 'three Rs' of the gospel are all needed in gospel preaching. In chapters 1 to 4 these are ruin, redemption and responsibility. In connection with man's ruin some say we should not emphasise sin but Romans establishes his guilt before God, 1. 18 – 3. 20. In connection with God's remedy, some say we should not preach the blood but Romans makes it precious, 3. 21-26. The responsibility to believe, 4. 1-25, sounds simple but it is necessary to remind ourselves of it. We must not add to it such things as the need for striving. A person is saved through faith in Christ alone.

After the flood there were three families in the earth, Shem, Ham and Japheth. Broadly speaking, Jews descended from Shem, black-skinned peoples from Ham and other Gentiles from Japheth. Each of these is brought to the bar of God in chapter 1 verse 18 through to chapter 3 verse 20.

(1) Man's Ruin
1. 18 – 3. 20

1. 18 – 1. 32 Unenlightened Nations
The sons of **Ham** are brought to the bar of God and **condemned on the grounds of creation**. Creation declares God, but they preferred not to know Him and changed the truth into a lie. They worshipped idols instead of the living God. Man becomes like the object he worships. He stoops lower than the beast of the field. Three times over in this section it is stated that God gave them up. He withdrew His restraining hand.

2. 1 – 2. 16 Enlightened Nations
The sons of **Japheth** are **condemned on the grounds of conscience**. They stood in condemnation of the unenlightened nations, yet did the same things! It has always been the shame of these Gentiles to do in secret what others did in public.

2. 17 – 3. 8 Jews
The sons of **Shem** are condemned **on the grounds of the covenant**. The Gentiles were judging others while doing the same things, but the Jews were boasting. They boasted the custodianship and teaching of the law and yet they broke it.

3. 9 – 3. 20 The Divine Verdict

All men are under sin. Note the use of 'none' four times. The whole world is guilty before God. The sentence of death has been passed on all mankind.

(2) God's Remedy
3. 21-31

This is a precious section in the Bible. The unique character of the present day should be noted where in chapter 3 verse 21 Paul says, 'But now' and in chapter 3 verse 26, 'at this time'. This refers to this unique day of grace and the wonders connected with it. The day of grace does not now belong to the realm of prediction, but to fulfilment and reality.

What is the remedy? God's provision now is that if man cannot be righteous in himself, He has procured for him a righteousness through the blood of Christ. Man, through faith, can be declared right for time and eternity.

(3) Man's Responsibility
4. 1-25

Man's responsibility is to believe. In this chapter David and Abraham, two Old Testament characters, are given as examples. In connection with **Abraham**, Genesis chapter 15 is cited, while, in connection with **David**, reference is made to Psalm 32. Why were these two men cited? Abraham believed God and it was counted to him for righteousness. This was before he was circumcised. David, however, believed God as a circumcised man. Thus, whether a person is a Jew or a Gentile, God's salvation is on the same terms.

Abraham was a good man, but that never saved him: faith was necessary. On the other hand David was a wicked man when he believed, but faith saved him. Abraham trusted the promises of God regarding the birth of his son, something which was naturally impossible. David trusted the mercy of God.

It is good to note the recurrence of the word 'blessed'. David had the happiness of forgiveness despite the magnitude of his sins.

(4) The Glorious Truth of Faith in Christ
Chapters 5-7

In **chapter 5, past guilt** is dealt with as the believer is justified; now the believer enjoys a **present standing in divine grace and future glory** is assured.

Chapters 6 and 7 go together. In chapter 6, the Christian is **free from sin** which is viewed as a master and a monarch. In chapter 7, he is **free from the law** which is viewed as a husband. That freedom has been brought about by the death of Christ. The Christian has died with Christ: he has **died to sin** to live to God and has **died to the law** to bring fruit unto God.

(5) Chapter 8

This chapter reveals the power for living to God, and bringing forth fruit for Him, namely the Holy Spirit. He is the pledge that I belong to God, gives power to live for God and is, further, the pledge of future glory.

CHAPTERS 9-11 DISPENSATIONAL

In **chapter 9** the apostle deals with Israel in the past, in **chapter 10** with Jews and Gentiles in the present and in **chapter 11** with the Jews in the future. In chapter 9, he speaks of his heaviness and constant sorrow of heart, whereas in chapter 10 he relates the desire of his heart, namely that the Jews might be saved. Psalm 19 is quoted in chapter 10 verse 17. The voice of creation is heard in the whole world and so it is with the gospel in the present day. 'Whosoever' is accordingly cited from the Old Testament.

In chapter 11, Paul deals with the Jews in the future. He speaks of Israel and a future for that nation. The word 'until' should be noted in chapter 11 verse 25. God will have taken out of the Gentiles the complement of the saved and will resume dealing with the nation.

CHAPTERS 12-16 PRACTICAL

In **chapter 12** the apostle speaks of consecration, in **chapter 13** of subordination, in **chapter 14** of toleration, in **chapter 15** of evangelisation and, in **chapter 16**, he records his salutation.

INTRODUCTION

Chapter 1 verses 1-17

vv. 1-6 The Messenger and the Message
In relation to both the messenger and the message, the apostle states three things. As to the messenger he was a **bondservant** of Jesus Christ, 1. 1, an **apostle**, 1. 1, and also an **evangelist**, 1. 1, 5. The order in which these are listed is of interest. Others might have mentioned last of all that they were servants but Paul is happy to be a bondservant of Jesus Christ. As to the message, he speaks of its **source** as being of God, 1. 1, its **subject** which is His Son, 1. 1, and its **sphere** which is all nations, 1. 5.

vv. 1-2   **Paul, a servant of Jesus Christ, called to be an apostle, separated unto the gospel of God, (Which he had promised afore by his prophets in the holy scriptures,)**

Paul was a **bondslave** by purchase, having been 'bought with a price', 1 Cor. 6. 20. As a result, he was God's peculiar possession, Tit. 2. 14; 1 Pet. 2. 9.

Each believer is a bondslave but not necessarily an apostle or an evangelist. In 1 Corinthians chapter 7 verse 22, 'he that is called, being free, is Christ's servant' and, in Ephesians chapter 6 verse 6, Paul, addressing bondservants, calls upon them to serve their masters, 'not with eyeservice', but 'as servants of Christ'.

A bondservant by purchase is to do with conversion. It is a move from the slavery of Satan to the slavery of God. He is bound now by the chains of divine love, doing the will of God from the heart. This is very practical teaching. A bondslave is one who acknowledges the Lord Jesus Christ as absolute Master. He is bound to serve: his will and abilities are wholly at the disposal of his Master.

The first *'doulos'* in the New Testament is found in Matthew chapter 8 verse 9 in the words of the centurion, 'I say to my *doulos* do this and he doeth it'. We must each ask, 'Is this true of me?' Obedience is not optional for the Christian.

Then, he was **an apostle** by calling. Notice that he was 'called an apostle' and that in verse 5 he had 'received apostleship'. In other books he describes himself as being called an apostle 'by the will of God', but here he simply states that he is divinely 'called'. High priests in the Old Testament were priests by succession. Apostleship was not like this: they did not succeed other apostles, nor were they either chosen by men or self-appointed. Thus, when he says, 'I am the apostle of the Gentiles', 11. 13, his sphere of service, not his ordination, is in view.

The word 'apostle' means 'sent one', and in Paul's case one officially sent of God. This speaks of authority. There are three kinds of apostles in the New Testament. There were apostles of Christ Jesus, apostles of the Lamb and apostles of the churches.

The apostles of Acts chapter 1 are 'apostles of the Lamb'. These were twelve in number. In relation to them, our Lord said, 'Verily I say unto you, that ye which have followed me, in the regeneration when the Son of man shall sit in the throne of his glory, ye also shall sit upon twelve thrones, judging the twelve tribes of Israel', Matt. 19. 28. Apostles of the Lamb have experience and ministry belonging especially to them. They are in the church, but their ministry is especially to Israel. In Acts chapter 8, after the stoning of Stephen, the apostles of the Lamb stayed in Jerusalem as a link between the church in its infancy and the nation of Israel. In the coming kingdom, the wall of the city has 'twelve foundations, and in them the names of the twelve apostles of the Lamb', Rev. 21. 14. We may conclude, therefore, that the choosing of Matthias was done in a correct manner: Christ was absent and the Holy Spirit was not yet given

In 2 Corinthians chapter 11, Paul refutes the claims of some that he was not an apostle because he had never seen the Lord, or that he was inferior to the twelve appointed on the mountain of the Beatitudes. They had seen the Lord. Paul points out that he had actually seen the risen Lord and though this was not a credential of apostleship it showed that he was not at all inferior. He says, 'For I suppose I was not a whit behind the very chiefest apostles', 2 Cor. 11. 5.

The apostles of Ephesians chapter 4 did not necessarily see the Lord; they were given by the ascended Lord and are apostles of Christ. Reference is made to the apostles of Christ, 1 Thess. 2. 6. Paul was one of these but, in addition, he had seen the Lord.

Paul was also **an evangelist** by separation. Paul had three separa-
tions. He was first of all separated from his mother's womb, Gal.
1. 15, reminding us of Jeremiah, to whom the Lord said, 'Before I
formed thee in the belly I knew thee; and before thou camest
forth out of the womb I sanctified thee', Jer. 1. 5. This was an act of
God. Then, he was separated 'unto the gospel', 1. 4. This was an
act of Christ separating him to a general work. The third separation of the apostle was an act of the Holy Spirit to a special work,
Acts 13. 2. Thus, the Godhead was involved in this threefold
separation.

The gospel is the gospel of God, 1. 1, and this can be seen in three
ways. In terms of its conception, the source was the heart of God.
We may recall the words of Acts chapter 28 verse 28, 'the salvation
of God'. In terms of its execution, God loved, God gave, God sent,
10. 6-8. The gospel is entirely of God. Man did not need to go up to
fetch Christ down nor to go down to raise Him up and, through
preaching, God brings His word to people to believe it. In terms of
its revelation, this, too, is of God and the verses from Galatians
chapter 1 verse 12 onwards indicate it was unique to Paul. The
words of 1 Corinthians chapter 15 verse 3 should be remembered,
'I delivered unto you first of all that which I also received'. Ephesians chapter 6 verse 19 speaks of the 'mystery of the gospel', truth
previously hidden in the heart of God but now revealed. It was
promised 'afore', but was not enjoyed. Abraham and Moses
became heirs of a promise which is realised as far as we are concerned. Abraham knew nothing of regeneration, for instance, or of
being in Christ, or being seated in heavenly places.

vv. 3-4   **Concerning his Son Jesus Christ our Lord, which
               was made of the seed of David according to the
               flesh; And declared to be the Son of God with
               power, according to the spirit of holiness, by the
               resurrection from the dead:**

The subject of the message is '**his Son**', 1. 3, and he reminds his
readers of His humanity and His deity. We needed a Saviour who
could lay His hand on both God and man. No mere man could lay
his hand upon God and for a man it would be a disaster if God laid
His hand on him. We required a Saviour in whom humanity and
deity is combined and this is true alone of Christ Jesus. A Saviour
who is not God would be like a bridge broken at the other end.
Our need is met in Christ.

'The spirit of holiness' is His own spirit. A spirit of holiness could not be in the presence of death, without exercising quickening power. The Saviour said regarding Lazarus' illness, 'This sickness is not unto death, but for the glory of God, that the Son of God might be glorified thereby', John 11. 4.

He was 'made of the seed of David according to the flesh', or 'flesh-wise', as to His humanity, but He was 'declared to be the Son of God with power . . . by the resurrection from the dead'. That He was of the seed of David scotches any idea that He was not a real man but it should be noted that the seed was a royal seed. In this letter, Paul wrote to Jews and Gentiles. The Jews had to acknowledge that He was of the seed of David in terms of His title to the throne. The Gentiles also had to acknowledge His deity. Both these ideas are found in Psalm 2. In respect of His being the seed of David, God says, 'Yet have I set my king upon my holy hill of Zion' and acknowledging His deity He says, 'Thou art my Son', Ps. 2. 6-7.

He was marked out distinctly by signs to be the Son of God with power. Thus, He was marked out to be what He always was by His raising dead ones. This is His life-giving power seen in operation. The next statement is not resurrection 'from' but 'of' the dead, so it is not His own resurrection that is in view but that of those whom He raised during His life on earth.

v. 5   By whom we have received grace and apostleship, for obedience to the faith among all nations, for his name:

'Grace and apostleship' is from Jesus Christ our Lord. He is an apostle by call, 1. 1, but his apostleship is here said to be what he has received from the ascended Lord. This links with Ephesians chapter 4 verse 11, 'He gave some apostles'.

'Grace' signifies equipment for service. This is not saving grace, but is connected with gift. The apostle himself was the gift and grace was the qualification, divinely given, to exercise it. The gift was not an office; it was exercised by grace. So, he speaks of 'the grace given unto me', which is his apostleship, 12. 3. Again, in 1 Corinthians chapter 3 verse 10, 'According to the grace of God which is given unto me, as a wise masterbuilder, I have laid the foundation', he is referring to his apostleship. While others may be instrumental in planting local churches, the apostle alone laid the foundation for every local church and he did this in exercise of his apostleship.

'**For his name**' is connected with receiving grace and apostleship. He 'received grace and apostleship for his name', that is, for His sake or in honour of all that He is.

Being possessed of deity, it was right that Paul should preach His Lordship, to which he alludes in verse 5 when he speaks of 'obedience to the faith among all nations'. This is the present sphere of the gospel, a point frequently made in the New Testament

The obedience of faith is the faith that brings salvation. Faith that saves is an act of obedience. In chapter 10 verse 3, he speaks of those who, in seeking to establish their own righteousness, 'have not submitted themselves to the righteousness of God'. The gospel requires a complete capitulation to the righteousness of God, 16. 26. There are examples in the New Testament, such as Saul of Tarsus saying, 'Lord, what wilt thou have me to do?' This is an acknowledgement of the lordship of Jesus. Again, the Philippian jailor asks, 'What must I do to be saved?' This is the obedience of faith. When we believed we came to an end of self and capitulated to God. The obedience which marked salvation's day should mark every day of my life. This is illustrated by Abraham in Hebrews 11, who was called and who obeyed. This obedience of faith results from the sovereign action of the Holy Spirit in dealing with us. So, in 1 Peter chapter 1 verse 2, the obedience of faith that saves is the result of a sovereign sanctifying work of the Holy Spirit. By nature man is a son of disobedience, as Ephesians and Colossians make clear, and it is only as the Spirit of God acts that man will believe.

v. 6   **Among whom are ye also the called of Jesus Christ:**

'**Among whom**' indicates that those to whom he writes were examples of the present sphere of the gospel. They were '**the called of Jesus Christ**' not as having been called 'by' Him, because the call is always connected with 'God,' but because they were called to become Jesus Christ's: it is the genitive of possession.

vv. 7-17 His Desire to see Them
In this section the apostle speaks of his desire to see them, vv. 7-12, and of hindrances to that desire being fulfilled, vv. 13-17.

The desire to see the Roman believers is expressed in verse 11 where he indicates to them that 'I long to see you'. Three things may be noted about that desire. When he speaks of serving with, or in, my spirit, 1. 9, he refers to the **spring of his desire**.

In that he served 'in my spirit', he indicates that it was not a mere duty. Rather, he serves worshipfully. This was not a mere vocation but was prompted by an inward, active, intelligent devotion. This called forth prayer, 1. 10, and caused a longing to see them, 1. 11.

Secondly, he alludes to the **occasion of his desire**. This was as he viewed them Godward, calling them 'beloved of God', 1. 7, and as he viewed them manward, in testimony to God, reminding them that 'your faith is spoken of throughout the whole world', 1. 8.

In relation to the **object in his desire**, the apostle states what he would do for them, to establish them, 1. 11, and what they could be to him, 1. 12. Paul never thought of himself as being above help from other saints. Further, it was that he 'might have some fruit among them', 1. 13.

v. 7   **To all that be in Rome, beloved of God, called to be saints: Grace to you and peace from God our Father, and the Lord Jesus Christ.**

The apostle speaks in a twofold way of those who are called. As **beloved** they were reminded of God's love and the fact that they were the objects of it. As **saints** they were reminded of God's nature and the fact that they were now suited to it.

God is the source of **grace**; **peace** is the result of grace and the channel through whom it is known is the Lord Jesus Christ.

v. 8   **First, I thank my God through Jesus Christ for you all, that your faith is spoken of throughout the whole world.**

There is a lot about **faith** in this chapter. In verse 5, faith obeys; in verse 8, it manifests itself; in verse 12, its power was felt by other saints and, in verse 17, faith is characteristic of the whole Christian life.

It might be asked as to how people can speak about a person's faith since it is between the soul and God. The answer is simply that faith was evident in their life, as it should be in the life of every believer. In their case their faith was evident in Rome where

Caesar was and had to be acknowledged as lord. However, its fame went beyond the city to the whole known world, that is, the Roman Empire. This is the significance of 'world', Acts 11. 28; 17. 6; 19. 27.

v. 9   **For God is my witness, whom I serve with my spirit in the gospel of his Son, that without ceasing I make mention of you always in my prayers;**

When the apostle states that he served God **'with (in) my spirit'** he speaks of something which only God could see. Thus, **'God is my witness'**. He was no hireling in the work of God. God knew of his prayers for them and his longing to see them, 1. 11. We should not be just pulpit men, serving in a professional way but rather we must have an active devotion of spirit and have the good and benefit of others at heart, even at personal cost. That his prayers were **'without ceasing'** is the product of his serving in the spirit: habitually he prayed for them. No doubt this would not be a mere cursory remembrance. Chapter 16 informs us that he knew their names, something made more remarkable by the fact that he had never been to Rome.

The verb **'serve'** here means 'to serve worshipfully', a different word from the one he employed in chapter 1 verse 1 and we do well to remember that service in the gospel is not for the purpose of entertainment but rather is an aspect of worship.

v. 10   **Making request, if by any means now at length I might have a prosperous journey by the will of God to come unto you.**

God was ordering his circumstances. It was not a safe journey, but one ordered by God. Chapter 15 verse 32 should be noted in this regard, where he urges the believers to pray for him that he 'may come . . . by the will of God'.

v. 11   **For I long to see you, that I may impart unto you some spiritual gift, to the end ye may be established;**

There are references in many epistles to Paul's desire and God's will. Sometimes God's will is different from what we think it might be. In Acts chapter 16 Paul and his company go to Philippi but are put in prison. In 1 Corinthians chapter 16 verse 9 he indicates that 'a great door and effectual is opened unto me, and there are many adversaries'. Opposition does not mean that we are moving outside of God's will.

Paul desired to impart unto them 'some spiritual gift'. The word, *charisma*, is used in chapters 5, 6 and 12 and is of wide significance, indicating fruit in their lives. He also desired to preach the gospel to saints and sinners at Rome. This would involve sound spiritual teaching.

v. 12   **That is, that I may be comforted together with you
           by the mutual faith both of you and me.**

In turn, they would be a help to him and so he speaks of 'mutual faith'. This does not, of course, refer to a trust in each other. In chapter 12 verse 3, it is 'according as God hath dealt to every man the measure of faith'. Each has a measure of faith according to which is the measure of his apprehension of the truths of God. The Faith is apprehended by faith. Mutual faith involves helping each other in what we apprehend of divine truth. Paul was not beyond being helped by others.

v. 13   **Now I would not have you ignorant, brethren,
           that oftentimes I purposed to come unto you,
           (but was let hitherto,) that I might have some fruit
           among you also, even as among other Gentiles.**

Paul now deals with the hindrances to the fulfilment of his desire to see them. We might ask why Paul mentions that he had often purposed to come unto them. Were insinuations being made regarding a motive for his not going, such as his being afraid? This was the case regarding the Corinthians, 2 Cor. 1. 8-18, and the Thessalonians, 1 Thess. 2. 18. In the case of Thessalonica he was hindered by Satan: as far as Corinth was concerned he was afraid to go there for the reasons stated at the beginning of the second epistle. In the case of Rome what hindered him from visiting was that he 'strived to preach the gospel, not where Christ was named . . . For which cause also I have been much hindered from coming to you', 15. 20-22. Thus, he was hindered by preaching where Christ was not named.

The apostle makes three statements dismissing any insinuation about his not going to them. In verse 14, '**I am a debtor**'; in verse 15, '**I am ready**'; and in verse 16, '**I am not ashamed**'. It is important to note that these are statements made against the background of unworthy insinuations against Paul.

v. 14   **I am debtor both to the Greeks, and to the**
            Barbarians; both to the wise, and to the unwise.

We may note that here Paul sees himself as a '**debtor**' to Jews and
Greeks, sinners in need of salvation. In chapter 8 verse 12, he is a
debtor to the Holy Spirit to be subject to His leading and, in chapter 15 verse 27, he is a debtor to the saints for the material help they
gave to him in affliction. The word he uses is a strong one. He felt
he owed it. He was under an obligation to pay and feels his
responsibility. It is clear, then, that this was no mere professional-
ism on Paul's part; rather, it was an obligation, a burden, a debt.

In 1 Corinthians chapter 9 verse 16, he states that 'necessity is laid
upon me'. He was a debtor to God to discharge a debt to sinners.
Notice, also, how in Ephesians chapter 6 verse 20 he makes reference to the fact that 'he ought to speak' to make known the
mystery of the gospel.

The Greeks were cultured and civilised: the Barbarians were the
opposite. To both, as well as to the wise and the unwise, Paul was
prepared to discharge his debt.

v. 15   **So, as much as in me is, I am ready to preach the**
            gospel to you that are at Rome also.

Paul is not only a debtor but he is '**ready**' and willing, to the full
extent of his capacity, to make Christ known to those who were at
Rome.

v. 16   **For I am not ashamed of the gospel of Christ: for it**
            is the power of God unto salvation to every one
            that believeth; to the Jew first, and also to
            the Greek.

Further, he was '**not ashamed of the gospel**' he would be preaching. The idea in the figure of speech employed is that a thing is
demeaned to increase its intensity. A further example is to be
found in chapter 4 verse 19 where Abraham 'being not weak in
faith' was, in fact, strong in faith, 4. 20. Paul is stating that it is actually an honour to make Christ known and therefore no blush of
shame would be on his cheek as he preached.

There is a play on words in this verse. 'Rome' means power, but
the gospel is the **power of God**. Salvation includes salvation of the
spirit, soul and body. It is a complete, full and final salvation
which, up until Acts chapter 28, was to the Jew first.

v. 17   For I am not ashamed of the gospel of Christ: for
          it is the power of God unto salvation to every one
          that believeth; to the Jew first, and also to
          the Greek.

In the gospel a 'righteousness from God is revealed'. The 'righteousness of God' is two-fold in Scripture, referring both to His
own intrinsic character and to a righteousness which He has procured for sinful men. There is a need to understand which is
which in each case. In chapter 3 verses 25 and 26 he speaks of
God's intrinsic character. However, in chapter 3 verses 21 and 22 it
is righteousness procured. This righteousness is offered on the
principle of faith (in contrast to the principle of works) to be
received by faith wherever it is found and those who are justified
continue to live on the principle of faith. It is important, then,
to note that Paul is dealing with how one can be right with God,
so it is not God's intrinsic righteousness that is in view here.

THE NEED FOR THE GOSPEL ESTABLISHED

Chapter 1. 18 – 3. 20

In this section the need for the gospel is established as the apostle demonstrates universal guilt. From chapter 3 verse 21 onwards he reverts to the subject of the gospel, expanding chapter 1 verse 17.

There has been a variety of interpretations of this section of God's word. Some see it that in chapter 1 verse 18 to chapter 2 verse 16 the Gentiles are in view and the Jew then comes before us in chapter 2 verse 17 to chapter 3 verse 20. Others see it that in chapter 1 verses 18-32 Paul treats of the Gentiles, then, in chapter 2 verse 17 to chapter 3 verse 20 the Jew is the subject, with chapter 2 verses 1-16 being transitional. Yet others see the heathen in chapter 1 verses 18-32, the moralist in chapter 2 verses 1-16 and the Jew in chapter 2 verse 17 to chapter 3 verse 20. E. W. ROGERS spoke of man in the gutter, 1. 18-32, man on the pavement, 2. 1-16 and religious man, 2. 11-32.

I like to view it in the following way. In **chapter 1 verses 18-32** the heathen, or the pagan, is in view and he answers to Ham. In **chapter 2 verses 1-16** the enlightened Gentile is before us and he answers to Japheth. In **chapter 2 verse 17 to chapter 3 verse 8** the Jews, Shem's sons, are the subject. Ham, Shem and Japheth were, of course, the three sons of Noah. After the flood, Genesis 10, the world was divided according to their families.

Then, in **chapter 3 verses 9-20** the divine verdict on all mankind, Jews and Gentiles, is that all are under sin. Notice, in this section the words 'none' and 'all the world'.

We may further observe that the heathen are condemned on the ground of creation, 1. 18-32. The enlightened Gentiles are condemned on the ground of conscience, 2. 1-16. They condemn the heathen, but practice the same things and so he addresses the conscience when he says, 'and thinkest thou', 2. 3, 4. The Jew stands condemned on the ground of the covenant, 2. 17-3. 8, the law of

Moses, of which he was the custodian, 3. 2. The Jew judged the
Gentile and boasted in his custodianship and teaching of the law,
yet broke it. Thus universal guilt is established.

Chapter 1 verses 18-32 The Heathen

It is important to remember that Paul, in this section, is dealing
with man prior to the gospel age. He is establishing the need of the
gospel. These verses do not apply to men now. This is important to
establish for a proper understanding, 2. 6-10.

In verse 18 wrath is revealed in the flood as the heaven is opened
up. In verse 19 God was revealed in creation up to the flood so
that the antediluvians were without excuse. In verses 20-32 God
was revealed providentially to men after the flood, as there was a
revelation of His everlasting power and divinity. Man's response
should have been as indicated in verses 21 and 25, glorifying God
and being thankful and blessing the Creator for ever.

The heathen's sin is two-fold. Ungodliness is impiety and is in relation to God: unrighteousness is sin in relation to fellow men. It was
expressed in that in verse 23 they changed the glory of God: in verse
25 they changed the truth of God and in verses 26-27 they changed
the natural use of both men and women. Note, in verse 29, that they
are filled with all unrighteousness. Three times we are told that God
is giving them up. This is a solemn statement in verses 24, 26 and 28.
Such drastic action was taken as all involve apostasy. In verse 24,
God gives them up to uncleanness. The lusts of their own heart
issued in uncleanness. In verse 26, He gives them up to vile affections, passions of dishonour, sin of a more degraded character. Then,
in verse 28, He gives them up to a reprobate mind.

v. 18   **For the wrath of God is revealed from heaven
against all ungodliness and unrighteousness of
men, who hold the truth in unrighteousness;**

Verses 17 and 18 are connected. In verse 17 there is the revelation
of righteousness and in verse 18 the revelation of **wrath**. The first
is made necessary because of the second; righteousness is needed
because of wrath revealed. The present tense 'is revealed' is used
in both verses and because of this some teach that this belongs to
the present age but I suggest that the grace of God is revealed now,
because the wrath of God is revealed as a fact and this really
relates to Old Testament times. It took place over and over again in
the Old Testament.

The 'wrath of God is revealed' does not refer to an emotional outburst but it is an abiding attitude connected with God's righteousness and speaks of His complete abhorrence of sin. The present tense 'is revealed' indicates a statement of fact which cannot be denied. Wrath is always connected with heaven; the flood, Sodom and Gomorrah, the vials and the Lamb appearing in judgement are examples of this. It is always revealed from heaven and though it may happen today it is the exception. Today is a day of divine patience. Paul speaks here of what cannot be denied.

'All ungodliness' means either that ungodliness is characteristic of all without exception or that it has reached its height. How impious! Man did not render to the Creator the gratitude that was His due. 'Unrighteousness' refers to the fact that they held the truth in unrighteousness. 'Held', hold down, suppress, is also used in chapter 7 verse 6. The truth that is suppressed is the truth that they know about the creatorial greatness of God. It is suppressed in unrighteousness as they lived unrighteous lives, acknowledging one God but permitting idolatry and stating that God's love is greater than His holiness and that He will not punish sin. Thus, there was an introduction of idolatry even though they knew God's greatness and majesty in creation. All the rest develops as a result of suppressing truth.

v. 19   **Because that which may be known of God is manifest in them; for God hath shewed it unto them.**

It is not everything about God that was manifested but that which might be known by man's apprehension. This is knowledge acquirable through nature rather than by revelation. '**That which may be known of God**' was revealed in them; not intuitively but 'among them'. The heathen had no excuse in ignorance. God showed, in creation, these things unto them in the sense that they were presented before their eyes.

v. 20   **For the invisible things of him from the creation of the world are clearly seen, being understood by the things that are made, even his eternal power and Godhead; so that they are without excuse:**

This could read 'from the world's creation the invisible things of him are perceived'. God is invisible but the invisible things of God, His majesty, power and wisdom, are now perceived and have been since the time of creation. There is sufficient proof in creation of the existence of God. It declares an ever existing and powerful being who is possessed of the attributes required to create. Every one who is honest with himself must admit a divine and infinite Creator. Matter is not eternal but the Creator has eternal, dynamic power.

'**Eternal**' occurs only here and in Jude 6 and has the thought of 'ever and always'. '**Godhead**' is not as in Colossians chapter 2 verse 9, 'in him dwelleth all the fullness of the Godhead bodily', but refers to what is characteristic of deity rather than to deity itself. As in Acts 17 it is the fact of His being rather than His personal attributes which is in view. The result is that people were thus without excuse. If people choose to be ignorant of the existence of God, it is not God who is blameworthy.

v. 21   **Because that, when they knew God, they glorified him not as God, neither were thankful; but became vain in their imaginations, and their foolish heart was darkened.**

Up to the end of the chapter the apostle speaks of God revealed providentially after the flood. Verses 21-27 speak of really degraded sin whereas in verses 28-32 the sin is less degraded but more pervasive.

The knowledge of God here is by revelation in creation. Man is capable of knowing God in terms of His existence but not in terms of John chapter 17 verse 3. The least that is expected of man towards the Creator is for man to glorify Him for His majesty and be thankful, for we depend on Him, but man ceased to thank and glorify God and gave it to the creature and to idols. Man should have '**glorified Him**' by acknowledging Him in a limited way as Creator but, in fact, he turned to the creature and, after the flood, to the idol. Man became like the idol.

The result was that men became '**vain in their imaginations**' and fell into folly in their thoughts. They weighed one idea against another in independent thinking. This was in fact morally wrong. They had then a '**darkened**', or senseless, unintelligent heart. Darkness is not just ignorance but spurious and depraved knowledge. They thus become more and more blinded.

v. 22   **Professing themselves to be wise, they became
            fools,**

They profess '**themselves to be wise**'. A kind of philosophy is in
view; they set aside divine revelation for their own speculation
and ability. The result was that '**they became fools**', Ps. 14. 1; 53. 1.
Corruption follows, for if men set God aside depravity follows.
Thus, in the Ten Commandments, the first five are Godward; the
second five are manward. Man questions what common sense
would accept and does not even recognise his folly.

v. 23   **And changed the glory of the uncorruptible God
            into an image made like to corruptible man, and
            to birds, and fourfooted beasts, and creeping
            things.**

This gives proof of their folly. They have a mean and foolish conception of God. God, who is spirit and eternal, must be
distinguished from the creation. To fail to acknowledge the infini-
tude of God leads to circumscribing God to the level of creatures.
The pride of man says nothing is greater than man and so God is
reduced to being lower than the level of men. Idolatry is always
linked with degraded behaviour. Anything that comes between
the soul and God in worship robs God of what is His due.

v. 24   **Wherefore God also gave them up to uncleanness
            through the lusts of their own hearts, to dishonour
            their own bodies between themselves:**

The setting in verse 23 is that man gives up God: in verse 24, God
gives up man. This is always the order in Scripture. God withheld
His restraining hand, not completely but so as not to restrain as
formerly. Men became like the beasts they worshipped. It was not
God who created the bad desires; they were there already. They
were not so much given up 'to' but 'in' the lusts of uncleanness.
There can still be such apostasy today when man gives God up. By
inference we may learn that God desires that we maintain the dignity of the human body in sanctification and honour.

v. 25   **Who changed the truth of God into a lie, and
            worshipped and served the creature more than the
            Creator, who is blessed for ever. Amen.**

Men changed truth into falsehood and this was the cause of
dishonour. It was changed as man compared the glory of the

incorruptible God and the glory of corruptible man. The **'glory of God'**, v. 23, is His essential and eternal being: the **'truth of God'**, v. 25, is in contrast to a lie. The truth is that He alone is to be worshipped. This truth is expressed in creation. The lie is the falsehood of idolatry. Man did not altogether reject the thought of a creator and might have even said their gods were inferior but it was still idolatry. **'Worshipped and served'** is always the order. In the term **'blessed for ever'** we learn that the creature's right attitude to God is a worshipful one. **'Amen'** is not just an affirmation: rather, Paul's heart was inspired to utter this.

v. 26-27   **For this cause God gave them up unto vile affections: for even their women did change the natural use into that which is against nature: And likewise also the men, leaving the natural use of the woman, burned in their lust one toward another; men with men working that which is unseemly, and receiving in themselves that recompence of their error which was meet.**

The apostle indicates the depths of sins to which man will go when given up by God. In this way the results of the sin of idolatry are shown. People speak of a new morality but God never changes. There is no limit to man's degradation when God is ignored. Note that this punishment is retributive.

v. 28   **And even as they did not like to retain God in their knowledge, God gave them over to a reprobate mind, to do those things which are not convenient;**

The sins mentioned to verse 32 are less degraded but more pervasive. It is not just men **'not liking to retain God in their knowledge'** but rather that they 'thought it not good to retain God in their knowledge' JND, RV. The knowledge of God met with no approbation so God gave them over to reprobation. The knowledge of God to which Paul here refers is knowledge through creation and providence. **'God gave them over to a reprobate mind'**. The thought in the word 'reprobate' is of being rejected after the test, refused, outcast, abandoned. This is a mind judicially blinded, unable to judge between right and wrong. That which is **'not convenient'** is that which is not becoming. Thus, having abandoned God and therefore having no right thoughts about Him, they have no right thoughts on the human level. Right behaviour amongst men has its source in God. He restrains the wickedness of the heart of man. When God gives up man He looses restraint.

What is happening in the world today is akin to this but here God is particularly showing the need which arose in Old Testament times for His moving in grace now. In 2 Timothy chapter 3 perilous times are characterised which are very similar to this. So, in the last days, man will give up God and go to idols of another kind.

v. 29   **Being filled with all unrighteousness, fornication, wickedness, covetousness, maliciousness; full of envy, murder, debate, deceit, malignity; whisperers,**

'**Unrighteousness**' heads the list of sins in these verses and covers all sorts of wickedness. '**Covetousness**' is overreaching; taking advantage. '**Maliciousness**' is evil in its largest sense: a disposition to injure and seek revenge. '**Full of envy**' signifies that there is no admixture of any virtue. Envy controls to the point of overflowing. This speaks generally of mankind. When God is abandoned there is no regard for life and so '**murder**' is included. This was especially the case with the slavery system. '**Debate**' is strife over words for vainglory, not to establish the truth. Men became full of **deceit** in conduct and full of **malignity**, having an evil disposition. This word has the thought of taking everything in the worst sense. '**Whisperers**' speak evil but it is communicated in secret, not in society. The accused thus has no means of defending what has been said about him.

v. 30   **Backbiters, haters of God, despiteful, proud, boasters, inventors of evil things, disobedient to parents,**

A '**backbiter**' is an evil speaker, even to the face. '**Haters of God**' are not just hateful towards God but the thought is of blaming God for every ill. These hate His holiness, justice and sovereignty. '**Despiteful**' is insolent, implying insult, contempt and reproach. It aims at attaching disgrace to its objects. '**Proud**' describes haughtiness. '**Boasters**' has in view ostentation. '**Inventors of evil things**' refers to unlawful pleasures. What means of doing evil are being devised! '**Obedience to parents**' is a duty taught even by nature: remember that Paul is speaking of people without the fifth commandment. It is nevertheless inscribed upon the heart of young people so that even the heathen are condemned for this.

v. 31   **Without understanding, covenantbreakers,**
          without natural affection, implacable, unmerciful:

Being **'without understanding'** is being foolish, void of understanding. They have understanding about the things of the world
but regarding God they usually are unintelligent. A **'covenant**
breaker' is faithless whether in personal relations with others or
business dealings. It has the idea of one who does not keep his
word. **'Without natural affection'** indicates that filial, parental
and marital affections are absent. **'Implacable'** and **'unmerciful'**
have no compassion for the distress of others and think nothing of
inflicting distress on them.

v. 32   **Who knowing the judgment of God, that they**
          which commit such things are worthy of death,
          not only do the same, but have pleasure in them
          that do them.

These know well the righteous ordinance of God's will. They
know what God requires and that God has ordained punishment
for wrong doing. The **death** referred to is not capital punishment
as not all preceding sins attract that sentence but these people
commit these sins habitually and the second death awaits them.
They also consent with those who so act. They have a seared conscience and delight in the moral ruin of others. They are one in
spirit with those who sin.

In our gospel preaching we must ensure that we establish universal guilt.

Chapter 2 verses 1-16 The Enlightened Gentile

In this section the enlightened nations stand condemned. Their
guilt was in judging others while doing the same things. It was
hypocrisy. A twofold error occasioned their guilt. Firstly, verse 3,
they had wrong thoughts regarding the judgement of God. They
persisted in sin because the judgement of God was delayed. This,
of course, is still true. Secondly, verse 4, they had wrong thoughts
regarding the goodness of God. In this connection it is not
'thinkest thou' as in verse 3 but **'despisest thou'**. They continued
in sin, remaining unrepentant, because of the richness of God's
grace being ever present with them. Many today also presume on
His goodness. In verse 5 the apostle concludes that by reason of
their hardness of heart they are unresponsive to God's goodness

and, further, because of their impenitent heart were amassing punishment to self. God's judgement is stated to be righteous, v. 6.

The next portion has difficulties. In it there are two kinds of men in view. There are those who seek for glory and others who are contentious. In the days prior to the gospel, times with which the chapter deals, God offered glory, honour, incorruptibility and eternal life. 'Glory' is a state of brilliance; 'honour' is praise; 'incorruptibility' is to do with a risen body on earth; and 'eternal life' is on this earth under the government of God. The terms of God's offer were 'patient continuance in well doing'. The thought is of unremitting patience in good works. This is, of course, the divine ideal which is set out here. Remember that until Calvary man was still under trial, under probation, and this verse refers to this. God did not offer, v. 10, what He could not give, and whether a man be Jew or Gentile it is 'the doers of the law' who shall be justified, v. 13. If a man could fully keep the law he would be justified just as if a man continued patiently in well doing he would be assured of glory, honour, incorruptibility and eternal life. To the contentious, however, the disobedient, those who disapprove of God's demands and His authority, who revolt against God's truth and obey unrighteousness by being a slave to evil, there is tribulation and anguish.

We have to await chapter 3 to discover God's verdict on all mankind. In verse 10 notice the repeat of 'none . . . none'. Though glory, honour, incorruptibility and eternal life was offered, v. 7, none could attain it for there was none righteous. Thus the need for righteousness is established.

v. 1   **Therefore thou art inexcusable, O man, whosoever thou art that judgest: for wherein thou judgest another, thou condemnest thyself; for thou that judgest doest the same things.**

In chapter 1 verse 32, people both do and have pleasure in them that do. In chapter 2 verse 1 people do and condemn those who do. They think their condemnation of others mitigates their guilt but it rather adds to it. The great shame of enlightened nations was to do in private what they condemned in public.

They were enlightened in that they had retained God in their knowledge and had not gone to idolatry. The apostle is not condemning them for the judging but for doing what they condemned in others. '**Same things**' does not refer to idolatry but to the sins of chapter 1 verse 26 onwards. Thus, they are inexcusable, without any excuse.

v. 2   **But we are sure that the judgment of God is according to truth against them which commit such things.**

'**We**' is apostolic. The judgement of God is according to reality and fact. There are no different standards with God from one person to another.

v. 3   **And thinkest thou this, O man, that judgest them which do such things, and doest the same, that thou shalt escape the judgment of God?**

'**Thou**' is emphatic. Paul is not actually addressing these people in verses 3 and 4 but is using rhetoric, as if they are in the dock. '**Thinkest thou**' is in respect of the judgement of God delayed in its execution. It is often the case that the greater the amount of personal sin there is, so much greater is the condemnation of others.

v. 4   **Or despisest thou the riches of his goodness and forbearance and longsuffering; not knowing that the goodness of God leadeth thee to repentance?**

The '**goodness**' of God is seen in the kindness and benefits He bestows. It is despised when man's heart becomes hardened by man supposing that God is overlooking sin because He has not intervened. Compare 2 Peter chapter 3 where the apostle Peter speaks of the longsuffering of God in salvation. An appreciation of this goodness leads to repentance. '**Forbearance**' is divine toleration in face of man's ingratitude. '**Longsuffering**' reminds us of God's slowness to wrath. '**Repentance**' is more than heart grief; it is a change of thought and will.

vv. 5-6   **But after thy hardness and impenitent heart treasurest up unto thyself wrath against the day of wrath and revelation of the righteous judgment of God; Who will render to every man according to his deeds:**

The heart of man is incurably perverse, enslaved to sin, and, in accordance with its nature, these men would not repent. Man's heart is marked by '**hardness**' though not as a result of present judgement: the judgement in the verse is future. Accordingly men were hoarding up 'wrath' so as to have an accumulation of it. That wrath will take effect in the 'day of wrath' when there will be displayed the absolutely righteous judgement of God. The 'day of wrath' is not a reference to the great white throne but the apostle is noting a contrast between the day of goodness and the day of wrath. It is not therefore 'the' day of wrath but 'a' day of wrath. We must not read into this passage all we know about God's future judgements, though Matthew chapter 16 verse 27 should be read in conjunction with verse 6. Paul here establishes the character of God's dealings as long as He deals with living men. The dead go to the great white throne.

Note should be made of the 'riches of his goodness' in verse 4, and the 'treasures of wrath' in verse 5. God offers abundant blessing and pardon but man amasses his own punishment. God treasures up all a man says, thinks and does against a day of wrath.

v. 7   To them who by patient continuance in well doing
            seek for glory and honour and immortality,
            eternal life:

We need to remember as we come to the next verses that the apostle is proving the need for the gospel. He is referring to days prior to the offer of grace in which man was on probation and in which the need for a righteousness from God was being demonstrated.

This verse speaks of those who by 'well doing' (good works) 'seek for glory', and 'honour' (approbation and praise from God). They expect to receive this by patient continuance. They also seek 'immortality' (incorruptibility): this is not unique to Christianity. There is no conjunction so the glory, honour and incorruptibility are viewed as the blessings of **eternal life**. This is not eternal life as we think of it in terms of John chapter 17 verse 3, which was manifested at the incarnation of God's Son, but eternal life as in the Old Testament, Dan 12; Ps 133, which was life for ever on earth under the government of God. This is what the rich young ruler had in view when he asked, 'What must I do to inherit eternal life?' To enter into eternal life he had to keep the commandments but the Lord Jesus Christ was showing that was impossible. A principle is thus established: in chapter 3 there is none that doeth good. In the Old Testament, as here, it was eternal life on earth, in a resurrection body, enjoying the government of God on earth that was in view.

'Patient persevering' in a good work is persevering in something that would try one's patience. 'Well doing' (good works) summarises the entire course of doing good. Blessing is assured to all who do this though none actually could, 3. 12. Continuance in well doing excludes failure. It is not just keeping the law in measure but in its entirety. Paul here speaks of that which God offered but which man could not attain. It is the divine ideal which man could not achieve. Zacharias and Elisabeth walked in all points blameless in respect of the ceremonial law, Luke 1, as did Paul, Phil. 3. God would have rewarded the complete keeping of the law but it is out of the reach of all.

(Cornelius was a man during the transitional period who was born again but who had not entered into the fullness of the eternal life we enjoy now. 'Worketh righteousness' in Acts 10 is the product of the faith which Cornelius had. Cornelius was in the old dispensation and not yet in the new. His righteousness and works were not self effort but evidence of the work of God in his soul.)

vv. 8-9   **But unto them that are contentious, and do not obey the truth, but obey unrighteousness, indignation and wrath, tribulation and anguish, upon every soul of man that doeth evil, of the Jew first, and also of the Gentile;**

Here is another example of the righteous judgement of God and the need for the gospel. In contrast to those who do good, there are those who do evil and, in contrast to incorruptibility and eternal life which would be the reward of the former, these verses speak of indignation, wrath, tribulation and anguish. '**Doeth**' is emphatic: it means 'practiseth' or 'worketh'. '**Wrath**' is God's attitude to those who do evil and '**indignation**' is the expression of it. '**Tribulation**' is experienced by man as the result of wrath and indignation and '**anguish**' is known when he finds he cannot help himself in this position.

This is universal in its application though it is to the **Jew first**. This is not in terms of time but because of the privileges and consequent greater accountability to God which the Jews had. Such punishment is promised because man here is **contentious** with God and does **not obey the truth** regarding God, cf. 1. 25. Further, he obeys '**unrighteousness**': this is sin in its largest sense be it moral, social, personal, or civil. Indeed, it is anything that violates what is right. It is to be noted that the order is as in chapter 1 where rejection of the truth leads to a wrong manner of living.

vv. 10-11   **But glory, honour, and peace, to every man that
            worketh good, to the Jew first, and also to the
            Gentile: For there is no respect of persons with God.**

The apostle returns to the teaching of verse 7 but adds '**peace**',
possibly as a contrast to 'anguish' in verse 9. In verse 9 there is no
respect of persons in terms of judgement, whereas in verse 10
there is no respect of persons in terms of acceptance. '**Glory**' is the
enjoyment of the presence of God: '**honour**' is the enjoyment of
the praise of God: '**peace**' is the enjoyment of the pleasures of God
which He bestows.

In verses 12-16, verses 13-15 are in brackets, Paul is explaining
what he has said in verses 9-11, that there is no respect of persons
with God in terms of both judgement and acceptance. So in verse 9
there is no respect of persons regarding judgement, whether Jew
or Gentile. In verse 10 the same applies in terms of acceptance,
whether of Jew or Gentile. Thus, in verses 12 and 16 the apostle
deals with judgement while in verses 13 to 15 he deals with acceptance, to show that in both matters God is no respecter of persons.
Verse 12(a) is directed to the Gentile, 12(b) to the Jew.

v. 12   **For as many as have sinned without law shall also
            perish without law: and as many as have sinned
            in the law shall be judged by the law;**

'**Without law**' has reference to a written law. God will not in judging him set before the Gentile the precepts set out in the Mosaic
law as these were never given to him. Thus, the omission of the
article should be noted; he speaks of the absence of a revealed or
explicit law, although the Gentile did have the law of conscience
which is dealt with later. No one is without a law, but here an
explicit law is in view. See verses 14 and 15 for what Paul has to
say about a Gentile law written by God in hearts.

'**Perish**' has in view eternal ruin, perishing in the final analysis.
This is not perishing arbitrarily with the written law being presented at the trial. The heathen will not be judged by light they
have not got, nor for ignorance of what had not been revealed to
them. They shall be condemned without the written law of Moses.
Outside of that law there is still sin and eternal ruin. If we were to
die without salvation we would not be judged by the law of Moses
but for sins in our life.

Those who have 'sinned in the law' or 'under the law' shall be 'judged by the law'. The Gentile perishes without law but the Jew shall be condemned by the law. Thus, condemnation will be determined by the law given to him. Note that this does not refer to the ceremonial law but to the moral law. Thus, God is righteous in His judgement.

v. 13   (For not the hearers of the law are just before God, but the doers of the law shall be justified.

Paul passes from judgement to acceptance. He shows that God is righteous whether in judgement or acceptance. It is the 'doers of the law' who shall be justified. Note the article: the law of Moses is in view and therefore the Jew who had that law. Hearing it does not justify the Jew: only the doer of it is 'justified'. (This is the first reference in the epistle to being justified.) 'Do' is continual and unremitting and this was the character of the law. 'Cursed is every one that continueth not in all things which are written in the book of the law to do them', Gal. 3. 10. If a man could render complete obedience to the law then he would be justified by such complete obedience. That was impossible, however. It could never be accomplished and this therefore shuts us up to salvation through Christ alone. 'No man is justified by the law in the sight of God', Gal. 3. 11.

v. 14   For when the Gentiles, which have not the law, do by nature the things contained in the law, these, having not the law, are a law unto themselves:

Paul is not speaking hypothetically and the use of 'when' is to be noted. He is not suggesting Gentiles do the law continually but do so at times. Gentiles do not have a written law but sometimes they do naturally or instinctively the things 'contained in the law' of Moses, cf. 1 Cor. 11. 14. This is not learned from an outside source, nor from Mosaic law, but naturally. Abel, Enoch and Noah had no law regarding sacrifices but offered them instinctively. Job and Elihu similarly had no law but did things contained in the law.

The expression 'a law to themselves' does not have the same meaning as when we say today that a person is 'a law unto himself'. Paul is not declaring Gentile morality but rather that on occasions such might act morally and responsibly. Gentiles have a moral code, a consciousness of what is right and wrong.

v. 15   **Which shew the work of the law written in their hearts, their conscience also bearing witness, and their thoughts the mean while accusing or else excusing one another;)**

This verse is not easy to understand at first but it explains the words of verse 14. Gentiles have a moral consciousness of right and wrong. They '**show**' to each other, objectively, the working of the law written in their heart, not by the way they live but by dealing with each case of right and wrong as it arises. There is a discussion among them and they either '**accuse or excuse**' them from the light which is in their hearts.

Note that it is the '**work**' (singular) of the law. This is not a reference to the precepts of the law of Moses but it is the law distinguishing between right and wrong. So in chapter 3 verse 20 the apostle will say, 'By the law is the knowledge of sin'. The work of the law is, metaphorically, '**written in their hearts**'. This is an important matter. God, as Creator, imprints on the mind and heart of the creature an understanding of what is right and wrong. Conscience is not always a safe guide. It is the faculty for judging oneself objectively and morally. This judgement is based on knowledge, conscience, of what is right and wrong but since it depends on knowledge it depends on many factors such as childhood training, influences in life, age, intelligence and memory. Thus, it is not always a reliable guide, but it can be purged, Heb. 9. 14. As Christians our consciences are to be adjusted by the word of God and then we will have a good conscience. A seared or cauterised conscience is one without feeling. Their conscience bears '**witness with**' or bears 'concurrent witness' with the law written in the heart.

The apostle speaks of the heart, **conscience**, and thought. 'Conscience' is a God-given sense of right and wrong: '**thoughts**' are to do with reasoning or reckoning one with another while the '**heart**', or mind is the capacity to think. 'Mind' and 'heart' are almost interchangeable though there is a difference as God says, I will write my law in their hearts and in their minds, cf. Jer. 31. 33 and Heb. 8. 10. The mind is the faculty of thinking while the heart is the faculty of knowing, understanding, or appreciating. This is a fine distinction. We have minds to remember the truth and hearts to appreciate it.

The expression 'accusing or else excusing one another', or 'one with another' in the sense of 'between themselves', has the idea of condemning or defending one another on the ground of conscience. To accuse or excuse supposes knowledge of right and wrong and it is conscience which gives that knowledge.

v. 16   **In the day when God shall judge the secrets of men by Jesus Christ according to my gospel.**

The parenthesis ends at verse 15. Paul now reverts from acceptance to judgement and this verse links to verse 12.

'In (the) day' has reference not to a specified time but to the certainty of it. Would that people would remember the day that is coming when God will judge! 'God will judge' and His will be the final assessment. In verse 15 the apostle has spoken of hearts, thoughts and conscience but in verse 16 of 'secrets'. There are no secrets to God. Light and darkness are alike to Him. It is not only the secrets that will be judged but the particular secrets mentioned here, bearing in mind that the enlightened nations are in view who practise secretly what they condemn publicly. Only God can judge the secrets. Men can escape human judgement by concealing deeds from other men but not so with God.

'According to my gospel' does not refer to the standard of judgement but indicates that the revelation of judgement is part of the gospel. Thus, the gospel includes the theme of judgement. Divine judgement will be executed by Jesus Christ as authority to judge has been invested by the Father in the Son of Man, John 5. 27. In Acts chapter 10 Peter speaks to Cornelius of 'Jesus of Nazareth ordained by God to be the judge of the quick and dead'. He is the One who will be on the great white throne.

Chapter 2 verse 17 — Chapter 3 verse 8   The Jew

In this section the circumcised Jew is in view. He was in covenant relationship with God who entrusted to him the law, which was intended to direct his life both morally and religiously. This was a great favour to the Jew. Big responsibilities were involved which should have humbled the Jew. However, the Jew was boastful and self confident. In chapter 2 verse 17 he became boastful of God, or boastful in God and boastful of the law, 2. 23. His boasting and self confidence was not that of a law breaker merely but of a hypocrite, with the result that not only was God grieved but His name was blasphemed among the Gentiles.

In chapter 2 verses 17-24, the apostle speaks of the Jew and the law. He boasted in it and taught it to others, yet he himself broke it. He rested in it, but with Pharisaic self righteousness, v. 17. He was instructed out of the law, v. 18, and had an outward form of knowledge of the law, v. 20, but he broke it, v. 23. Jewish guilt increased as instruction in the law made a Jew able to know God's will and to teach it to others, vv. 21-22. As being instructed in the law the Jew was personally able to know God's will and to approve the things that are more excellent, v. 18. Thus he was personally confident as to his ability to help others. He was '**teaching**' the law in the rabbinical schools, v. 21, '**preaching**' it in the synagogues, v. 21, and '**saying**' it in general converse on the law, v. 22, yet all the while he was breaking it.

In chapter 2 verse 25-29 he has in view the Jew and circumcision. Circumcision was the outward symbol distinguishing Jew and Gentile. Further, it was intended to give evidence of covenant relationship with God but it gave no advantage if the person was a law breaker. For this reason the Gentile, if he keeps the law, even though he is uncircumcised, is reckoned for circumcision, v. 26. The uncircumcised by nature, if he fulfils the law will stand in condemnation of those who by the letter and circumcision transgress the law, v. 27. Thus, the apostle makes clear that the mere outward Jew, though he is proud of it, is nothing and as for circumcision it is only a rite. '**A Jew inwardly**' means a Jew in a spiritual sense and connects with spiritual circumcision. Note the play on words: Judah means praise and the word '**Jew**' comes from that word. Paul then speaks of the praise of God. Even though he might be despised, one who is a Jew spiritually will have the praise of God, v. 29.

In chapter 3 verses 1-8 the apostle vindicates the character of God from a two-fold standpoint. In these verses he speaks of the faithfulness of God and the truthfulness of God, vv. 3, 7. Thus God is faithful and truthful.

Regarding the faithfulness of God the apostle asks, '**What if some (Jews) did not believe?**' He has in view the faithfulness of God in respect of His promises. Paul goes on to say in verses 4-6 that God will be faithful to His promises, but at the same time He must be faithful to His righteous character. In verse 4, God's righteousness must be vindicated by man's confession of sin and God's justice must prevail when He is under question. In verse 5, if man's unrighteousness, when it is confessed, vindicates God's righteousness, is God unrighteous who inflicts wrath? Perish the thought! You Jews accept God will judge the world. Though you are complacent and feel secure, says Paul, God will and must judge it but only a righteous God can do this. Summing up, Paul simply says 'Don't you see that God will be faithful to His promises regarding the future and that He is faithful to His righteous character now as far as sin is concerned?'

The apostle speaks regarding the truthfulness of God in verse 7. Paul may be accused of falsehood (evidently that was the case) but how can this be true, he asks, if through my deceit, or my lie, I have established the truthfulness of God in the matters of His promise and His righteous character, and that to His glory? Why yet am I judged as a sinner? Paul does not enter further into the slander in verse 8 but says that the doom of those who so speak is as just as it is sure for this serious perversion.

v. 17   **Behold, thou art called a Jew, and restest in the law, and makest thy boast of God,**

'**Thou**' is emphatic indicating an element of pride or personal glory in being '**called a Jew**', 'bearing the name of Jew'. The Jew was **resting in the law** as a foundation and **boasting** in God in a 'holier than thou' attitude. Thus, they personally despised others, an attitude exemplified in the man who prayed, 'I thank thee that I am not as other men are'.

The first mention of 'Jew' was after the division of the kingdom. The term was used in a specialised sense regarding the tribes of Judah and Benjamin but here it is used in a technical sense of the whole nation.

v. 18   **And knowest his will, and approvest the things that are more excellent, being instructed out of the law;**

Paul adds to the guilt of the Jew who had advantage over the Gentiles in **knowing His will**, the will of God contained in the law. '**Approvest**' has the idea of testing or approving: the Jew was able to put to the test what was right or wrong and to sort out moral problems, having the oracles of God. All this adds to the guilt of the Jews. Note that the Jews are not condemned here on the grounds of what they should have been as a priesthood but as being custodians of the law.

**v. 19   And art confident that thou thyself art a guide of
the blind, a light of them which are in darkness,**

Pharisaic **confidence** has always marked the Jew. In **'leading the
blind'** they guided those who were in darkness. No doubt this
was intended for the nation of Israel but this was boastful self-con-
ceit, for in practice he did not really do this. Those in darkness are
Gentiles: they 'sit in darkness and under the shadow of death'.

**v. 20   An instructor of the foolish, a teacher of babes,
which hast the form of knowledge and of the
truth in the law.**

As an **'instructor'** the Jew was a corrector of the foolish and a
teacher of babes. The Jew was confident that he could do both but
he only had a **'form of knowledge'**; an outward form as distinct
from inward power, a mere outline with nothing filled in. The
word has the same sense as in 2 Timothy chapter 3 verse 5 where
the apostle speaks of a 'form of godliness'. He is not charged here
with misapprehension but with an empty apprehension. He knew
the law and its rightness but it was to him without inward power.
Paul emphasizes he knew it but had no sincerity to back it up.

**v. 21   Thou therefore which teachest another, teachest
thou not thyself? thou that preachest a man
should not steal, dost thou steal?**

The Jew knew the law said 'thou shalt not steal' and taught it, but
did not act in accordance with it. His apprehension therefore was
an empty one: he did not apply it to himself and so it was bereft of
inward power.

There is a difference which ought to be observed between **'teaching'** and **'preaching'**. (We have failed in assembly life to
distinguish these gifts: not all preachers are teachers and not all
teachers are preachers.) Teaching took place in the schools while
preaching was in the synagogues and to the public at large. The
teacher applied his knowledge to others but not to himself. It is
good to aspire to be a teacher but do not read the word just to be
able to teach others: read to be taught yourself and to feel its sharp
edge in your own life. The preacher proclaimed to others but disobeyed himself. Paul applies these facts to the whole nation.

v. 22   **Thou that sayest a man should not commit
         adultery, dost thou commit adultery? thou that
         abhorrest idols, dost thou commit sacrilege?**

'**Sacrilege**' is not the idea of robbing heathen temples of their
idols. The Jew would keep apart from the heathen and his temple
and would never set foot in it during the day lest he be defiled.
However, he would think nothing of creeping in at night to steal
from them. Thus, he abhorred the idols of the heathen but bowed
down to the idol in his own heart namely the idol of the love of
gain. He would bend his scruples to augment his possessions.
Accordingly, sacrilege here is not so much the idea of robbing temples of idols but robbing them of valuables kept there. This was
hypocrisy. He abhorred idols in his teaching but would steal for
his own advantage. It is easy to have an idol in the heart, especially the love of wealth and possessions.

v. 23   **Thou that makest thy boast of the law, through
         breaking the law dishonourest thou God?**

Boasting in the law but **breaking** it was true not just of the teachers and preachers but of the whole nation in day to day converse.

v. 24   **For the name of God is blasphemed among the
         Gentiles through you, as it is written.**

'**As it is written**' refers to Ezekiel chapter 36 verses 20-23 which
relates to the Jews in captivity among Gentiles. 1 Timothy chapter
6 verse 1 warns that it is possible for the Christian servant so to
behave towards his master that the name of God is blasphemed.
We need to feel this in our own hearts.

v. 25   **For circumcision verily profiteth, if thou keep
         the law: but if thou be a breaker of the law,
         thy circumcision is made uncircumcision.**

There is a warning in this and the next verses against the Jew
accepting the outward symbolic mark of circumcision with no
regard to its inward meaning. '**Circumcision profits**' if one is a
doer of the law, but otherwise it becomes uncircumcision. There
was a profit in circumcision for it gave the Jew access to the oracles
of which he was a custodian but there was no profit if the law was
not kept.

v. 26   **Therefore if the uncircumcision keep the
          righteousness of the law, shall not his
          uncircumcision be counted for circumcision?**

If the '**uncircumcision**' keep the righteous requirement of the law
(that is, upon conversion, 8. 3), his physical uncircumcision is
reckoned for spiritual circumcision.

v. 27   **And shall not uncircumcision which is by nature,
          if it fulfil the law, judge thee, who by the letter
          and circumcision dost transgress the law?**

Natural '**uncircumcision**', the Gentile, would then '**judge**' the Jew
who '**transgresses the law**'. '**By letter**', or 'with' letter, refers to the
Jews' means of knowing the law. Circumcision in these circumstances is a meaningless badge.

v. 28   **For he is not a Jew, which is one outwardly;
          neither is that circumcision, which is outward in
          the flesh:**

To be '**outwardly**' a Jew is nothing: to be circumcised and yet to
be divorced from the significance of circumcision is equally of
no value.

v. 29   **But he is a Jew, which is one inwardly; and
          circumcision is that of the heart, in the spirit, and
          not in the letter; whose praise is not of men, but of
          God.**

To be a Jew '**inwardly**' refers to that which is hidden: it is '**of the
heart**', in contrast to one who is a Jew manifestly in verse 28. This
is the circumcision that is vital and such is praised by God.

Chapter 3 verses 1-8   The Jew   (continued)

v. 1   **What advantage then hath the Jew? or what profit
          is there of circumcision?**

The apostle here begins his vindication of God's character in
respect of which verses 1-2 are introductory. His mention of 'advantage' relates to the question of the superiority of the Jew in
terms of privilege. The truth of the closing verses of the previous
chapter is that a Jew is one who is one inwardly and that circumcision of heart is what matters.

v. 2   **Much every way: chiefly, because that unto them were committed the oracles of God.**

There is advantage '**much every way**'. See chapter 9 verses 4-5 for a list of many great advantages. '**Chiefly**', or first of all, however, the '**oracles of God**' were committed to them. This was the law: see Acts 7, Hebrews 5 and 1 Peter 4 for other usages. The law is spoken of as the oracle, or divine utterances, even though it was written. This is because it had a voice that must be heard and obeyed. Hebrews chapter 12 verse 25 refers to 'him that spoke on earth'. Though written it was initially spoken so that the law was the actual spoken words of God. In fact decalogue means ten words. By 'first of all' Paul has in mind that this was the matter in which they particularly stood or fell before God. Thus, it was the most important. When the covenant was given the people were sprinkled with blood, Exod. 24. 8, indicating that if the law was broken it would mean the death of either the sinner or a sacrifice. Israel was the sole custodian of God's oracles for the world.

v. 3   **For what if some did not believe? shall their unbelief make the faith of God without effect?**

'**For what**' is the formula of argument. '**Some**' was actually the majority and the unbelief to which he refers relates to the time when the promised Messiah was here. However, their unbelief will not make the faithfulness of God in respect of promises given to the nation of Israel without effect. God will be faithful to the promises given to the nation even though some did not believe.

v. 4   **God forbid: yea, let God be true, but every man a liar; as it is written, That thou mightest be justified in thy sayings, and mightest overcome when thou art judged.**

'**God forbid**' means 'far be the thought'. 'Perish the thought!', says the apostle, that God would be faithless in respect of the promises given to the nation of Israel. Indeed, '**let God be true**'. Let God be worthy of all credit: do not question His veracity. Whoever else may be false let not God be false: He will fulfil His promise. God would indeed be false if He did not fulfil His promise and yet some today say there is no future for Israel nationally. God is true to His promise notwithstanding the unbelief of the nation at large.

'**That thou mightest be justified in thy sayings**' is quoted from Psalm 51 verse 4. The sayings are God's sayings and it means that man must acknowledge that God does not change in any of His sayings. David acknowledged this in Psalm 51 by confessing his sins, recognising that God is faultless. The expression 'mightest overcome' in Psalm 51 speaks of God coming into judgement when someone disputes with Him. Paul is here saying that God must overcome in justice. Paul speaks not of God accusing man but man daring to accuse God. Thus, it is not God overcoming in judgement upon the guilty but rather that when anyone disputes with Him He must prevail. In verses 3-4 God is true and there is no falseness with Him; men must acknowledge this or never know God's forgiveness, for man can never argue with God and prevail.

v. 5   **But if our unrighteousness commend the**
          righteousness of God, what shall we say?
          Is God unrighteous who taketh vengeance?
          (I speak as a man)

Psalm 51 verse 4, cited in the preceding verse, is the confession of sin: this is acknowledging that God is true and all else is false and this brings forgiveness. In this verse it is the matter of '**our unrighteousness**' showing forth the '**righteousness of God**'. Our unrighteousness confessed, as in Psalm 51, shows off the righteousness of God. That is just the gospel and, if that is true, is God unrighteous who inflicts wrath? In the Greek, because of the interrogative particle, the question is asked in such a way as to expect the answer 'yes'. Just as God was not unrighteous at the flood or at Sodom and Gomorrah, so He is not unrighteous when He inflicts wrath. When Paul says, '**I speak as a man**', he is indicating that it is from the merely human standpoint: to question God is to speak according to men.

v. 6   **God forbid: for then how shall God judge**
          the world?

The opposition expected an affirmative answer but Paul is quick to defend God's honour with this strong denial. No! Perish the thought! '**How shall God judge the world**' if he is unrighteous? Paul is appealing to Jews who believed God would judge the world. If the argument were true, that God is unrighteous, He would have to abdicate as judge of the world.

To summarise, unbelief did not alter God's faithfulness to His promises in verse 3 and, in verse 5, God's saving the unrighteous does not make Him wrong in inflicting wrath upon the unrighteous who fail to confess.

v. 7   **For if the truth of God hath more abounded
         through my lie unto his glory; why yet am I also
         judged as a sinner?**

The apostle asserts that God is true in the sense that He is truthful. The contrast is not between truth and error but Paul has in mind truthfulness in contrast to falsehood. It speaks of what is genuine both in His promises and forgiveness.

In using the expression '**through my lie**' Paul is speaking in respect of the charge made against him, which was that he was false when he preached the gospel and that man's unrighteousness could show forth the righteousness of God. His detractors thought of this as his deception.

When Paul asks, '**Why yet am I also judged a sinner?**', he is not thinking of his fellow Jews judging him but rather of judgement from God. My preaching means this: as a sinner I must be judged. As a man apart from the grace of God I was a sinner and I must be judged. However, he says, I am no longer a sinner. In fact the gospel he preached abounded to God's glory in the matter of salvation.

v. 8   **And not rather, (as we be slanderously reported,
         and as some affirm that we say,) Let us do evil,
         that good may come? whose damnation is just.**

In verse 7 Paul says, 'I accept I must be judged', and therefore, in verse 8, it could not be true that he is saying let us do evil that good may come. Paul is saying that judgement and not good is the lot of the sinner.

Thus, there was this injurious charge; Paul says it is completely erroneous. Then, he adds, '**whose damnation is just**'; the damnation of such is just because they have made a solemn assertion that God is unrighteous. Paul is saying that God is righteous both in forgiveness and in judgement.

Chapter 3 verses 9-18 The divine verdict on all mankind
The Jew is no better than the Gentile. Verses 10-12 speak from a negative standpoint while in verses 13-17 it is seen from a positive standpoint. Man is devoid of righteousness, of intellectual faculty regarding God and of desire after God, vv. 10-12. Then the whole

48   ROMANS

man is exposed as being in the service of sin, vv. 13-17. In verses
13-14 he is exposed from the standpoint of his corruption, reference being made to his throat, tongue, lips and mouth. In verses
15-17 he is exposed from the standpoint of his violence with reference to his feet, way and ways. The apostle's conclusion is that
there is no fear of God.

Then, in verses 19-20, there is Paul's final conclusion. 'Every mouth'
is stopped, the 'whole world' is guilty. There are no exceptions.

v. 9   **What then? are we better than they? No, in no
            wise: for we have before proved both Jews and
            Gentiles, that they are all under sin;**

All are 'under sin', both Jew and Gentile, in Adam. All have fallen
under it and are subject to it. This verse really speaks of the divine
verdict on the Jew but the Gentile is condemned too from the
standpoint of showing that the Jew is no better than the Gentile.
Thus, in the condemnation of the Jew there is also the condemnation of the Gentile. If Paul was referring to the Jew only, he would
speak of him being under the curse of the broken law but as he
speaks of Gentiles also he says that all are 'under sin'.

v. 10   **As it is written, There is none righteous, no, not
            one:**

Here is a general description of man's ruin. 'There is none righteous', a statement especially pointed to the Jew. Literally, it says,
'There is not a righteous man, not even one'. There is not a man who
conforms to the claims of God. This statement is not in the Old Testament but introduces Old Testament quotations which follow. This
verdict is, of course, not accepted by the self-righteous.

v. 11   **There is none that understandeth, there is none
            that seeketh after God.**

The apostle here speaks of intellectual ability not in a general way
but from a moral standpoint, being an ability to make right judgements. Ephesians chapter 4 verse 18 speaks of men having 'the
understanding darkened'. Thus, there is no movement of the natural heart toward God. Adam, having sinned, hid from God. The
first question in the Old Testament is, 'Where art thou?' By way of
contrast, the first question in the New Testament is, 'Where is He?'
The doctrine of the gospel is in these chapters and one must start
by explaining man's utter ruin before God.

v. 12   **They are all gone out of the way, they are together become unprofitable; there is none that doeth good, no, not one.**

'**All gone out of the way**' is citing Isaiah chapter 53 verse 6. All have wandered from the ways of God and from paths of righteousness. To be '**unprofitable**' is to be worthless as far as God is concerned. A man's highest and noblest efforts before God are unprofitable if he is still in his sins. '**There is none that doeth good**': not one person unremittingly practises goodness, no, not so much as one.

v. 13   **Their throat is an open sepulchre; with their tongues they have used deceit; the poison of asps is under their lips:**

In these verses there is a detailed account of man's sin in word and deed. In verses 13-14 his sin is in word and in verses 15-17 his sin is in deed. Psalm 5 verse 9 is quoted. It is not 'their throat is a sepulchre' but '**an open sepulchre**'. Man's throat is like an open grave emitting stench and corruption. This suggests the heart is the sepulchre and the throat its open door. Our Saviour said that from the heart proceeds all kinds of evil, Mark 7. 21. Their **tongues** employ deceitful words. They are not just evil words but deceitful, words that cannot be taken at face value. The '**poison of asps**', citing Psalm 140 verse 3, suggests that just as the asp conceals poison until the moment of use the sinner keeps at the ready slanderous words that would sting and poison.

v. 14   **Whose mouth is full of cursing and bitterness:**

The apostle now cites Psalm 10 verse 7. Their mouths are '**full of**', ready at any moment to spill over, '**cursing**' against God and '**bitterness**' against man.

v. 15   **Their feet are swift to shed blood:**

This citation comes from either Proverbs 1 or Isaiah 59. The first man to be born proved the truth of this statement. This is especially true under provocation when he will quickly take vengeance.

v. 16   **Destruction and misery are in their ways:**

'**Ruin and misery**' follow from verse 15 in the train of feet swift to shed blood.

v. 17   **And the way of peace have they not known:**

'**The way of peace**' is spoken of in a general sense both with God and fellow man.

v. 18   **There is no fear of God before their eyes.**

Citing Psalm 36 the apostle states not simply there is 'no fear of God' but that there is '**no fear of God before their eyes**'. Their eyes are not focused on God but on self. Thus, they have no reverential fear of God.

v. 19   **Now we know that what things soever the law saith, it saith to them who are under the law: that every mouth may be stopped, and all the world may become guilty before God.**

Here, then, is the divine conclusion on all mankind. We have already seen the idolatrous Gentile condemned on the ground of creation, the enlightened Gentile condemned on the ground of conscience and the Jew condemned on the ground of the covenant.

Those '**under the law**' are Jews and proselytes. The law has condemned the Jew. Now every mouth is stopped, as all are guilty. There is no defence or excuse. Job chapter 40 verse 4 says, 'Behold, I am vile; what shall I answer thee? I will lay mine hand upon my mouth'. Thus is the mouth stopped but when the mouth is stopped the ears are opened. It is a grand thing when this happens in the day of grace! To hear the gospel is to hear of judgement because of guilt but also of divine grace, God's provision for all mankind. In the day of judgement there will be no defence, excuse or hope of escaping eternal judgement.

v. 20   **Therefore by the deeds of the law there shall no flesh be justified in his sight: for by the law is the knowledge of sin.**

'**No flesh**' means no human being. The **knowledge of sin** has been gained as the law exposes sin in its true character.

GOD'S REMEDY

Romans chapter 3 verses 21-31

Up to chapter 3 verse 20 the apostle Paul has established the utter ruin of man. Every kind of man has been brought to the bar of God and all have been found guilty. All are without excuse or defence. Now, in chapter 3 verses 21-31, God's remedy for ruined man is brought before us. There is only one remedy and it is the death and blood of Jesus Christ.

The apostle now enters on the great truth of justification. In this passage, justification is viewed from the standpoint of God the justifier. In chapter 4, it is viewed from the standpoint of the justified. In chapter 5, the blessings consequent upon justification are brought before us.

It is important to note the word '**now**' at chapter 3 verse 21 and the expression '**at this time**', 3. 26. The apostle establishes that the time of expectation is over and now God is moving out to justify the guilty. The '**righteousness of God**' is not God's character here but refers to a means of being right with God which God has procured and which He now offers to the guilty. Divine justice has provided justification for sinners, a justification consistent with God's righteous character.

We learn in the New Testament that the guilty are justified by God, justified in Christ, justified by faith, justified by grace and justified by blood. If to purify means to make pure and to sanctify means to make holy, to justify simply means to make just. A just God can make the guilty sinner just in His sight. This is 'a righteousness from God'.

In this section Paul contrasts God's dealings in the past and in the present. The righteousness of God is no longer merely predicted but it has been manifested and it is by faith. '**Now**', v. 21, is the climax of privilege as far as men and women are concerned. Noah preached righteousness, one that God demanded: Paul preached righteousness, one which God has provided.

There are three subsections in this main section. In verses 21-23 the apostle speaks of the difference between witness and manifestation. Then, in verses 24-26, he treats of the difference between the remission of sins in the past and the justification of sinners now. Finally, in verses 27-31, there is the difference between works and faith.

Further, in verses 21-23, he speaks of the righteousness of God in connection with the law and the prophets. Two expressions are to be noted: **'without law'** and **'by the law'**. Then, in verses 24-26, he speaks of the righteousness of God in connection with the Day of Atonement as he thinks of propitiation. Finally, in verses 27-31, he speaks of the righteousness of God in connection with the works of the moral law.

v. 21   **But now the righteousness of God without the law is manifested, being witnessed by the law and the prophets;**

That the righteousness of God (the means of being right with God) was **'manifested'** means that it was made open to view. The same word is used in 2 Timothy chapter 1 verse 10, 'now made manifest'. This was formerly witnessed but now it is open to view. It was witnessed by the law and the prophets, showing the importance of both prophetic and typical teaching. It was witnessed in the law typically and in the prophets prophetically. **'The law'** refers to the Pentateuch in which types and sacrifices portray that man can only be right with God on the ground of sacrifice. **'The prophets'** refer to such as Isaiah in particular and perhaps the apostle has before his mind such passages as, 'I bring near my righteousness', Isa. 46. 13, and 'by his knowledge shall my righteous servant justify many', Isa. 53. 11. *Jehovah Tsidkenu*, the Lord our righteousness', is a name of God taken from Isaiah 51. Man has no righteousness in self; he must look to the Lord. Righteousness and faith are linked with both the Pentateuch, Gen 15. 6, and the prophets, Hab. 2. 4. It is now no longer witnessed; it has come.

This is a righteousness of God **'without the law'** as being independent of the law that offered no hope to guilty man. It is excluded now and with it law-works as a means of justification. The law could only expose man's unrighteousness and it condemned him. Man had no standing before God by means of the law. This means of being right with God is wholly different from the terms contained in the law for it is purely by grace. There is a complete exclusion of any works of man. These statements are also in Galatians. What the law could not do God has provided and He has provided it now.

Paul is thinking in this verse particularly of the Jew. The law was introduced not to prove man a sinner but to give sin its true character as rebellion. Thus, when the apostle dismisses law as a ground of salvation, he would encompass all mankind.

v. 22   **Even the righteousness of God which is by faith of Jesus Christ unto all and upon all them that believe: for there is no difference:**

This righteousness of God's providing is '**by faith of Jesus Christ**'. This expression is also in Galatians chapter 2 verse 17. Paul is not speaking of the personal faith of the Lord Jesus Christ. The genitive is objective and is therefore 'faith in Jesus Christ': He is the object of faith. The contrast is between the works of the law and the faith of Jesus Christ. There is no justification by the works of the law but by faith which has Jesus Christ as its object. In the same way, 'the faith of the Son of God', Gal. 2. 20, is 'faith in the Son of God'.

The '**righteousness of God**' is '**unto all**' in its direction and '**upon all**' in its bestowal. Also, it is towards all in terms of its offer and upon all in terms of its benefits. The righteousness of God is based on the Lord Jesus Christ's work and offered on that basis. It is the means whereby the sinner can be made right with God, 2 Cor. 5. 21. God made Him to be what by no process He could ever become that we might be made in Him what we could never otherwise be. Righteousness is thus reckoned to the believer. It is offered to all on the ground of propitiation and is upon all them that believe on the ground of substitution. '**Upon**' is upon as a shelter from the storm: when faith is put in Christ this righteousness is upon them as a shelter. Note that this is not the righteousness of Christ but the righteousness of God secured by the death of Christ.

There is '**no difference**' between Jews and Gentiles. All who believe on Jesus Christ are looked on by God as righteous.

v. 23   **For all have sinned, and come short of the glory of God;**

In stating that '**all have sinned**' Paul indicates that all need the righteousness which is offered unto all. He looks upon the whole human race; not as being in Adam, 5. 12, but the human race viewed as a whole and every individual in it.

'**Come short**' is in the present tense. It is the same word as is used in connection with the prodigal: he began to be 'in want'. Also, Paul uses it of himself when he says, 'I know how to suffer need', Phil. 4. 12. It is also in Hebrews chapter 11 verse 37 where it is translated 'destitute'. Thus, sinners are destitute of '**the glory of God**'. This is exemplified in Belshazzar who was weighed in the balances and found wanting. The idea is not that man has fallen short in terms of representing God here but has fallen short of being suited for God's presence. He falls short in terms of divine requirements. The glory of God filled the Tabernacle and it had to be veiled by the veil. Even on the Day of Atonement that glory had to be covered, as did the High Priest. Had the High Priest entered the holiest without that glory being covered it would have slain him – so he was covered with the cloud of incense. Also, to Moses God said, 'Thou canst not see my face'.

The glory of God, then, is His holiness and His requirements. Man is totally destitute of this. Our Saviour, as man, is the glory of God in the sense that He revealed that glory. Thus, to fall short of God's glory is more than falling short of the law: it is falling short of God's glory as fully revealed in the perfect Man.

v. 24   **Being justified freely by his grace through the redemption that is in Christ Jesus:**

The apostle here speaks of the difference between remission of sins in the past and justification now.

What a full verse this is! Three matters in particular are dealt with. These are the efficacy of the work of Christ, the gracious character of God and the fact that the sinner is undeserving. These are three important ingredients in the presentation of the gospel.

'**Redemption**' is setting free by paying a price. The price was paid and we are justified gratuitously. In fact, a judicial price was paid by which the demands of God were met. In Job chapters 9 and 25 the question is asked as to how man should be just. Here is the answer: it is only because of Calvary. God cannot overlook sin and therefore a price must be paid. Thus, a just God deals righteously with man's sin. To move in mercy at the expense of justice would mean God is no longer God. This, then, is the work of Christ.

Paul now speaks of the character of God: He justifies 'by his grace'. 'Grace' always relates to God's disposition. In 2 Corinthians chapter 9 and Hebrews chapter 2 grace is in the person of Christ but here God's disposition to the sinner is in view. Justification is an act of favour and of grace. This is unmerited and is bestowed 'freely', or 'without a cause'. The thought is that it is without price or cost. The word is used often in the New Testament, John 15. 25; 2 Cor. 11. 7. In 2 Timothy chapter 3 Paul preached the gospel freely, without a charge. The sinner is totally unworthy and justified without a cause and for nought. In that it was without a cause, we were guilty: in that it was for nought, we were bankrupt and could not pay.

Verse 24 concludes on the 'redemption that is in Christ Jesus' and Paul goes on to amplify this in verse 25, having the Day of Atonement as the background.

v. 25   **Whom God hath set forth to be a propitiation through faith in his blood, to declare his righteousness for the remission of sins that are past, through the forbearance of God;**

'Whom' refers, of course, to Christ Jesus. He has been 'set forth' to view. The mercy seat was in the Old Testament hidden behind curtains but now Christ is set forth to the view of all.

'Propitiation' is the word for 'mercy seat'. This was the lid of the ark in the holiest of all. The ark contained the tables of the covenant. Cherubim looked down on the lid of the ark, which was God's throne. It only became a mercy seat when the blood of an animal, slain at the brazen altar, was sprinkled upon the throne of God. God said, 'And there I will meet with thee, and I will commune with thee from above the mercy seat, from between the two cherubims which are upon the ark of the testimony', Exod. 25. 22. God meets and communes with the sinner on the ground of blood shed: this satisfies the claim of the divine throne. After the fall of man the cherubim stood between God in His righteous character and man in his guilt. In Genesis 3 the cherubim wielded the flaming sword. Man could not approach God. Now, however, there are the cherubim on the throne of God and there is no flaming sword. Instead of wielding that sword to keep man out, they gaze upon the blood which has satisfied the claims of God's throne enabling God to meet with man.

The King James Version suggests the ground of justification is faith 'in his blood'. The comma ought not to be put after 'blood'. Faith is linked with propitiation and blood is linked with the declaration of His righteousness. We are not called upon to put our faith in the blood but in the person. Our faith in a living Saviour enables God to reckon to us the value of His blood. Thus, Paul speaks not so much of faith in His blood but of the believer (faith) in Jesus.

The mercy seat of old was a visible, tangible, golden seat on which was sprinkled the blood of animals but our mercy seat is through faith. It is a living Saviour before God in all the value of His blood shed on Calvary. The sons of Beth Shemesh took the lid off the ark. Their sin was not curiosity but really that they looked on the unbroken tables of the covenant. No one could see these and live for they demanded every man's death but God says He will meet us on the ground of shed blood.

There are three words for propitiation in the New Testament. In 1 John chapters 2 and 4 the person who is the propitiation is in view. In Romans chapter 3 and Hebrews chapter 9 the place where God and men meet is in view while in Hebrews chapter 2 the thought is of the work of propitiation.

Note the two phrases relating to time in this and the next verse namely **'the remission of sins that are past'** and 'at this time'. 'Sins past' means the sins of the old economy committed prior to Calvary. On the Day of Atonement divine justice was not fully satisfied by animal sacrifice. God might have punished their sins but He did not. God moved in forbearance and remitted their sins because of the blood on the mercy seat. **'Remission'** is found only here in the New Testament. In Matthew chapter 26 and Hebrews chapter 9 it is really 'putting away' but here it is 'passing over'. The blood of Old Testament sacrifices did not satisfy divine claims but because of it God moved in forbearance and it allowed Him to go on with men at that time. When God moved in forbearance He did so in view of Calvary. When the blood was shed at Calvary, God's righteousness was declared in His going on with men prior to Calvary despite the inefficacy of the sacrifices. Blood in the Old Testament had no inherent value but it looked on to the blood of Calvary. The blood of the Old Testament was only a temporary measure. God had no pleasure in the sacrifices nor did they accomplish His will, Hebrews 10, but God honoured them in that they spoke of Christ. Notice, in this connection, the words of Hebrews chapter 9 verse 15 where the writer speaks of 'the redemption of the transgressions that were under the first testament'.

v. 26   **To declare, I say, at this time his righteousness: that he might be just, and the justifier of him which believeth in Jesus.**

'**At this time**' is not just making a contrast to a past day but refers to a time that was fixed in divine purpose – this unique era in which we live. It has the same sense as in Romans chapter 5 verse 6, 'in due time'. Two things characterise God's dealings in the past day and the present day. In the past, God showed forbearance and passed over sins, but in the present He is not moving toward us on grounds of forbearance but as a just God on the basis of the sacrifice of Calvary. He does not now merely pass over our sins or forgive them but justifies the guilty person. Divine justice has been satisfied: man's case has been dealt with righteously.

vv. 27-28   **Where is boasting then? It is excluded. By what law? of works? Nay: but by the law of faith. Therefore we conclude that a man is justified by faith without the deeds of the law.**

From this verse to the end of the chapter the apostle establishes that the law of a past day was not made void by the principle of justification. He points out that that law has in fact been established. There are two references to law in verses 28 and 31. Paul establishes that faith and law are mutually exclusive: man's failure to keep the law made justification by faith the only way by which the sinner could be made right with God. He goes on to say that since it is by faith there can be no boasting on man's part.

In these verses, '**boasting**' is excluded. Paul has already said in chapter 2 verse 17 that the Jew is a boaster in the law and in God. Here the Jew boasts in his former position but Paul shows that if justification is by works, there is personal merit. If there were personal merit there is room for boasting but this is not so if it be by faith alone. Glory, then, is given alone to God. So, boasting has been '**excluded**'.

The '**law of works**' is the Mosaic law, a general principle of works enjoined on man for acceptance before God. The '**law of faith**' concerns the fact that God has enjoined that faith alone is the principle by which man could be accepted before God. Thus, the 'law of faith' is just the principle of faith being the ground of man's acceptance. There can be no mixture between works and faith. Justification is outside the sphere of law keeping and therefore, in verse 28, justification is 'without deeds of law'. In Romans, Paul establishes faith, without works. In Galatians, the error was not works to the exclusion of faith but works in addition to faith. In Galatians, false teachers taught circumcision as an undertaking to keep the whole law in order to be saved, but this verse establishes there can be no mixture.

v. 29   **Is he the God of the Jews only? is he not also of the Gentiles? Yes, of the Gentiles also:**

Paul introduces the fact here that God is the God of the Jews and the Gentiles. He does so because once justification by faith, apart altogether from the deeds of law, is accepted then it is realised that God is God both of Jew and Gentile.

v. 30   **Seeing it is one God, which shall justify the circumcision by faith, and uncircumcision through faith.**

That there is one God is a great truth of the Old Testament. Now the apostle states that there is '**one God**', the same God who justifies both Jew and Gentile. In Galatians 2, Paul and Barnabas were given the right hands of fellowship in connection with the fact that the same gospel was to be preached by Peter to the Jews and by Paul to the Gentiles.

Both Jew and Gentile would understand that justification is by faith, but no word of Scripture is insignificant. The apostle now states that for the circumcision justification is '**by** (*ek*) **faith**' and for the uncircumcision it is '**through** (*dia*) **faith**'. In that it is by or 'out of' faith it is not out of the law. It is by faith, or on the principle of faith, as opposed to the principle of law works. The Jew was given the law: he would be accepted if he could keep the law. Now, says the apostle, it is no longer on the principle of law but 'by' faith. In that it is 'through' faith it must be remembered that the law was not given to the uncircumcision and so here there is no comparison with what was true at another time. The idea is 'on simple exercise of faith'.

v. 31   **Do we then make void the law through faith?
          God forbid: yea, we establish the law.**

Paul anticipates an objection, possibly by the Jews, that the law is annulled through faith. This is not at all the case as the law is in fact established. Christ did not bring justification by meeting the requirements of the law in his life but by His meeting the demands of the broken law in His death. The law proved man guilty and deserving of judgement to be executed either on the delinquents or their substitute. Calvary has vindicated the law for there was One who met, for the Jew, particularly, the demands of divine justice as stated in the law. Thus, justification establishes the law in the sense that its demands have been fully met.

MAN'S RESPONSIBILITY

Chapter 4 verses 1-25

In chapter 4 man's responsibility is to exercise faith. Two characters are cited. The first is Abraham with reference being made to Genesis chapter 15 verse 6 where the first mention of faith is found in the Bible and was in respect of the promise of a son. The second character is David with reference being made to Psalm 32 verses 6-8.

Abraham was the friend of God, a good man, yet he needed faith. David was a wicked man yet God justified him. Abraham believed God before his circumcision, which was in Genesis 17. David believed when he had been circumcised and so we learn that whether in circumcision or uncircumcision it must be by faith. In Genesis 15 Abraham trusted the promises of God while in Psalm 32 David trusted in the mercy of God. The chapter may be divided as follows:

In verses 1-5, the apostle speaks of **the object of faith** and cites Abraham who believed God.

In verses 6-8, he speaks of **the blessedness of faith** and cites David who also believed God.

In verses 9-10, he speaks of the **sufficiency of faith** which in verse 9 avails both for circumcision and uncircumcision.

The **succession of faith** is the subject of verses 11-16: in verse 11 Paul speaks of the father of all who believe.

In verses 17-22, the **nature of faith** occupies the apostle as he speaks of Abraham who believed God who quickens the dead and who against hope (from the human standpoint) believed in hope (from the divine standpoint) being not weak in faith.

Lastly, he draws the **lesson of faith** in verses 23-25 as the historical narrative is seen not to be written for his sake alone.

Alternatively the chapter may be viewed in the following way:

In verses 1-5, in speaking of Abraham, Paul illustrates the principle on which one is justified.

In verses 6-8, David is an illustration of the kind of people God justifies.

Then, in verses 9-16, Abraham is again mentioned to show that the offer of justification now and the promise of future inheritance are to both the Jew and Gentile.

In verses 17-25, the illustration of Abraham is still before the apostle, as he shows not merely the terms of justification but the testimony which must be accepted. This testimony concerns death and resurrection. He believed God who quickens the dead: we believe in God who raised the dead.

v. 1   **What shall we say then that Abraham our father, as pertaining to the flesh, hath found?**

The words 'as pertaining to the flesh' are linked to 'our father' not to 'hath found'. Thus, Paul addresses the Jew in particular. The apostle is concerned with what Abraham 'hath found' in terms of acceptance before God.

v. 2   **For if Abraham were justified by works, he hath whereof to glory; but not before God.**

Abraham had nothing to glory in 'before God'. 'Before God' means 'toward God': the thought is of looking God in the face. Abraham could never glory there.

v. 3   **For what saith the scripture? Abraham believed God, and it was counted unto him for righteousness.**

The testimony of Scripture is employed and Genesis chapter 15 verse 6 is cited. Abraham put a personal trust in God and his faith was 'counted unto him for righteousness'. 'Counted' is 'reckoned', as in 4. 4, 9, 10, a business term meaning 'to put to his account'. Faith was the condition, not the basis, of his justification. It is important to observe that in the Old and New Testaments the basis of justification is not faith but the blood of Calvary. Faith is not therefore the basis of Abraham's justification but, when he believed God, he was in the condition in which God was prepared, in anticipation of Calvary, to justify him. We saw in chapter 3 verse 25 that Calvary has declared God righteous in passing over sins of people like Abraham who, before Calvary, had faith in God

In Romans chapter 10 verse 17 we learn that faith cometh by hearing. Abel heard that the ground of acceptance was sacrifice. Abraham heard that he would have a son in his old age. He abandoned all hope in self, in human nature, and put his trust wholly in God. We too must abandon all hope in self and must put our unreserved trust in God.

Paul is not teaching righteousness in exchange for faith for that would make faith meritorious, which it is not. God has not saved me because I have exercised faith but because of Calvary; the basis of salvation is Calvary alone. Thus, his faith was not counted 'for' but 'unto' (*eis*) righteousness. In this connection see Romans chapter 10 verse 10 also. Through the exercise of faith God put righteousness to his account. The righteousness imputed to Abraham was not the reward of his faith; it was the reward of Calvary, in anticipation, imputed to him because of his faith. This is a most important matter.

Abraham became righteous in Genesis chapter 15 verse 6. Circumcision was the seal of his righteousness in chapter 17 but added nothing to it. Before Genesis 15 he was a man of faith, Heb. 11. 8, but the point is that the faith of Genesis chapter 15 verse 6 was faith which totally abandoned trust in self and put its whole trust in God. Genesis 15 is, therefore, saving faith which though not a scriptural expression expresses a scriptural thought.

v. 4   **Now to him that worketh is the reward not reckoned of grace, but of debt.**

'**To him that worketh**' refers to the person who works for salvation and relates to the works of the law. To work is to claim to be righteous. Work involves the principle of obligation on God's part: the law was a contract and if it was kept God was obliged to bless. Thus, God would have been under obligation to any who kept the works of the law but, as we have previously seen, no one did.

v. 5   **But to him that worketh not, but believeth on him that justifieth the ungodly, his faith is counted for righteousness.**

'**To him that worketh not**' for his justification '**but believeth on him**', his faith is counted for righteousness. '**Ungodly**' means 'impious'. The faith of such is the sole condition of justification and a principle is thus set out. Grace is unmerited favour. It must be noted that in James 2 works are as an evidence of salvation and, in that chapter, James cites Genesis 22 where Abraham's works were evidence of the faith of Genesis 15. Therefore, faith is the sole condition of justification.

v. 6 **Even as David also describeth the blessedness of the man, unto whom God imputeth righteousness without works,**

The apostle now introduces **David** to show the kind of people God justifies, namely the ungodly. There is no doubt that Paul's reference to the ungodly in verse 5 leads him to think of David in verses 6-8. Mention is made of David's iniquities and sins in verse 7 so here is something a little different. In Abraham is illustrated the principle of justification without works whereas David knew justification despite his evil works.

In these three verses we have brought before us the blessedness of the justified. In verse 6 the thought is of the happiness of righteousness imputed, in verse 7 of forgiveness enjoyed and in verse 8 of sin not imputed at any time.

The word '**also**' tells us that David now declares, as Moses did with regard to Abraham in writing Genesis 15. Abraham knew God's grace but David knew His mercy. With regard to Abraham the apostle asks in verse 3, 'What saith the scripture?' In verse 7, David also pronounces in Scripture. Abraham had the testimony of the Scriptures and in verse 6 we hear David's personal testimony.

v. 7 **Saying, Blessed are they whose iniquities are forgiven, and whose sins are covered.**

'**Iniquities**' involve lawlessness and are wilful. Where there is confession there is forgiveness. '**Sins**' can be done ignorantly, however, and these are atoned for or covered. In this verse, there is forgiveness and atonement. In Psalm 32, David goes on to say 'and in whose spirit there is no guile' and this is in the matter of confession.

v. 8 **Blessed is the man to whom the Lord will not impute sin.**

David here speaks of happiness through the knowledge of non-imputation of sin. '**Not**' means 'not at all', 'in no wise', 'not at any time' and is good for time and eternity.

v. 9 **Cometh this blessedness then upon the circumcision only, or upon the uncircumcision**

also? for we say that faith was reckoned to Abraham for righteousness.

'Blessedness' leads the apostle back to Abraham and he shows that the offer of justification now is made to both Jew and Gentile. It is not confined to those of the circumcision.

v. 10   **How was it then reckoned? when he was in circumcision, or in uncircumcision? Not in circumcision, but in uncircumcision.**

Faith was reckoned to Abraham in Genesis 15 before his circumcision in Genesis 17, a period of fourteen years later. Circumcision made no contribution to his justification.

v. 11   **And he received the sign of circumcision, a seal of the righteousness of the faith which he had yet being uncircumcised: that he might be the father of all them that believe, though they be not circumcised; that righteousness might be imputed unto them also:**

Circumcision in Genesis 17 was the sign of God's covenant but here Paul speaks of it as being a '**seal**' of His righteousness. He believed God while he was uncircumcised and thus became the '**father of all**' who believe whether in circumcision or otherwise.

v. 12   **And the father of circumcision to them who are not of the circumcision only, but who also walk in the steps of that faith of our father Abraham, which he had being yet uncircumcised.**

The term '**father of circumcision**' refers to spiritual circumcision which is true separation to God, whether a person is physically circumcised or not. It should be noted that in Galatians chapter 4 verse 23 the expression 'before faith came' does not mean that there was a time when no faith was necessary but the apostle speaks of the time before which the Lord Jesus was the unique object of faith. Thus, he speaks there of faith which has for its object Jesus Christ.

The '**steps of that faith of our father Abraham**' does not refer to steps in the Christian pathway: the clause has in view all those who exercise the faith that Abraham exercised. This is not a process for the individual but relates to the dispensation. The writer enlarges on this in verses 17-22.

v. 13   **For the promise, that he should be the heir of the world, was not to Abraham, or to his seed, through the law, but through the righteousness of faith.**

The thought is of the **'promise'** of the future inheritance. It is not only justification by faith that is in view but also heirship. This goes back to Genesis chapter 12 verse 3, 'In thee shall all families of the earth be blessed'. The promise by faith cannot be nullified whereas promise by law would be conditional.

v. 14   **For if they which are of the law be heirs, faith is made void, and the promise made of none effect:**

If heirship is by law, faith is made void. **'Law'** and **'faith'** are mutually exclusive. If it is by law, a legal contract is involved: this would make promises conditional.

v. 15   **Because the law worketh wrath: for where no law is, there is no transgression.**

Since the **'law worketh wrath'** because of **'transgression'**, it only produces in man what calls down the wrath of God. Inheritance by the law would therefore cancel out promise.

v. 16   **Therefore it is of faith, that it might be by grace; to the end the promise might be sure to all the seed; not to that only which is of the law, but to that also which is of the faith of Abraham; who is the father of us all,**

The promise is by **'faith'** that it might be by **'grace'**. It is of faith on man's part and by grace on God's part. Thus, the promise is **'sure to all'** the seed, not being imperilled by any condition of law. Abraham is the **'father of us all'** as the exemplar of the kind of faith that justifies.

v. 17   **(As it is written, I have made thee a father of many nations,) before him whom he believed, even God, who quickeneth the dead, and calleth those things which be not as though they were.**

From here until verse 22 the apostle treats of the nature of faith. Abraham believed **'before him'**, in His presence. Not only was righteousness imputed to him when he had none but also the promise was given to him when he could promise nothing in return. He believed in 'God who quickeneth the dead'. That which was dead which God quickened was, of course, Sarah's womb and this resulted in the birth of Isaac. The promise in Genesis chapter 17 was that he would be the father of many nations. Not only was there no nation then but he did not even have a son. God speaks of things that are not as though they were. We see this in Romans chapter 8 verse 30: 'whom he called he . . . glorified'. The apostle indicates that this is already done as far as God is concerned! As far as we are concerned it has not yet happened but God can call things as though they did in fact exist. God is outside of time and so is able to do this. It is in the light of this fact that we are to understand that we were chosen in Christ before the foundation of the world.

If the promise was by the law, human effort was required: it would have all depended on man. In the matter of faith, divine promise and imputed righteousness, however, both man and human effort are set aside. Just as it was with Abraham, the trust must be wholly in God and His resources.

v. 18   **Who against hope believed in hope, that he might become the father of many nations, according to that which was spoken, So shall thy seed be.**

There are two interesting statements in this verse, namely '**against hope**' and '**believed in hope**'. Against hope on the human side, he believed in hope from the divine side. Here is the pattern of faith. On the human side all was hopeless, but against hope Abraham believed in hope. The promise given was beyond hope if Abraham had reasoned as far as he and Sarah were concerned, that is, from the human side, but he believed in hope. Simply, he put his trust in God's word. This was an implicit and unswerving trust. The promise was not just that he would have a son but that he would be the father of many nations. At first, Abraham thought that this promise was not unconditional. Hagar was brought in and the result was Ishmael but he had to wait until the time of God's promise and he believed in hope. Abraham was asked to believe in something humanly impossible but he rested with confidence in God's promise. It is the same with us in the present day.

The connection between faith and hope should be observed. Hebrews chapter 11 verse 1 says, 'Faith is the substance of things hoped for'. Faith substantiated in Abraham's heart the hope that God had given him. There, in Hebrews 11, he looked for a city. Here, it is in respect of a son. In chapter 5 verse 2, the apostle speaks of a present faith and a future hope.

Abraham is the '**father of many nations**', of all them that believe. This refers, then, not only to the physical seed but also the spiritual.

v. 19   **And being not weak in faith, he considered not his own body now dead, when he was about an hundred years old, neither yet the deadness of Sara's womb:**

This verse has been rendered in two different ways. Some say that it should read 'considered' while others think that it should be '**considered not**'. The weight of authority is divided as to whether to retain 'not' or to exclude it. In fact, from a certain standpoint, both renderings are true. If 'not' is omitted the significance is that Abraham did not slight the obstacles: he took account of the obstacles. If 'not' is retained the significance is that Abraham paid no heed to the fact that his body was dead. Thus, both are right: he had faith that would overlook or slight the obstacles.

In considering this verse, we must take both Romans 4 and Hebrews 11 into consideration. Romans chapter 4 speaks of the deadness of Sarah's womb but Hebrews chapter 11 speaks of Abraham being as good as dead. These are two different statements. It is true that Sarah's womb was dead but, as far as Abraham was concerned, he was 'as good as' dead. Faith must look away from self to God.

Accordingly, he believed in hope, he considered not his own body now dead and he staggered not, he did not waver, he was fully persuaded. These are all remarkable statements especially in view of his great age at the time. Of course, the overall picture is in view, not instances where he appeared to waver.

v. 20   **He staggered not at the promise of God through unbelief; but was strong in faith, giving glory to God;**

Abraham was '**strong in faith**', if not in body, giving God the glory. Though the promise was given Abraham had his part to play and so 'strong' implies the part Abraham had to play in the promise, a part he would not have played had his faith been weak.

v. 21   **And being fully persuaded that, what he had
          promised, he was able also to perform.**

Abraham was '**fully persuaded**' in divine ability to perform the
promise. A question arises as to Abraham laughing. Abraham's
laugh was different to Sarah's. Sarah's was a laugh of contempt but
Abraham's was a laugh of incredulity.

The faith that justifies characterises every step of the pathway, see
chapter 1 verse 17. The faith that called Abraham out sustained
him all the way. This should have been the case when Peter got out
of the boat: the faith that enabled him to get out of the boat should
have remained and held him up on the water.

Abraham is the '**father of all**' in terms of his being our exemplar.

v. 22   **And therefore it was imputed to him for
          righteousness.**

We have seen that Abraham abandoned all trust in self to trust in
God and the word He had spoken and that this is the kind of faith
that enables God to reckon a person righteous. This is something
we have to do continually in our gospel preaching: we need to
emphasise this trust in God and His word. Man's proud, religious
heart thinks he has a part to play and he finds it hard to abandon
all trust in self but he must do this in order to be justified.

v. 23   **Now it was not written for his sake alone, that it
          was imputed to him;**

This verse commences the last section of the chapter in which Paul
speaks of the lessons of faith. That which was written was not
written for Abraham's '**sake alone**', nor merely for our informa-
tion but that we might have the same kind of faith. Abraham
believed and we believe.

v. 24   **But for us also, to whom it shall be imputed, if we
          believe on him that raised up Jesus our Lord from
          the dead;**

Abraham believed God as the God of promise: we believe God as
the God of fulfilment, the One who has '**raised up Jesus our Lord
from the dead**'. We believe not in a God who will do but who has
done. What is in view here is the faith that enables God to reckon
us righteous. Without faith it is impossible to please God,

whatever dispensation we are in. Even Old Testament sacrifices had to be brought in faith to be valid.

v. 25   **Who was delivered for our offences, and was raised again for our justification.**

This verse amplifies the end of verse 24. Jesus our Lord was '**delivered up**' as a victim for (*dia*: because of) our offences. The same word is employed in Romans chapter 8 verse 32, 'delivered him up for us all'. He was '**raised again for our justification**'. He was delivered up: our offences were put away. His being raised up is the divine side, the proof that we are declared just in the sight of God. Justification is secured by His blood as chapter 5 will teach us. His resurrection is the proof of God's acceptance of His justifying work. He was raised not to procure our justification but on account of it, as conclusive proof of its acceptance. Thus, no glory attaches to self: all glory is due to God.

THE GLORIOUS RESULTS OF JUSTIFICATION

Romans chapters 5 – 7

Chapter 5 is divided by the two words 'therefore', v. 1, and 'wherefore', v. 12. Verses 1-11 relate to the individual: verses 12-21 relate to the race.

We have seen that there is a three-fold division of this epistle, namely chapters 1-8, 9-11, and 12-16. In chapters 1-8 there are two subsections: in chapter 1 – chapter 5 verse 11 the subject is 'sins' while in chapter 5 verse 12 – chapter 8 verse 39 it is 'sin'. Thus, verse 11 is the conclusion of this section. Each section of the book ends with a note of praise: 5. 11; 8. 38-39; 11. 36; and 16. 27.

Chapters 4 and 5 are clearly linked. Chapter 4 ends with reference to our justification and chapter 5 starts, 'Therefore being justified'. In fact, chapter 5 sums up the section from chapter 3 verse 21 – chapter 4 verse 25 in which God is 'just, and the justifier of him that believeth in Jesus'. Now, in chapter 5 verse 1, Paul speaks of 'being justified'.

There are two matters we may note. Divine justice has been satisfied, v. 1, and divine love has been shown, v. 5. Note also that three times in the chapter Paul uses the verb 'exult' as he speaks of joy. In verse 2 we joy in God's future glory for us; in verse 3 we joy in God's present ways with us; and in verse 11 we joy in God Himself.

In Romans 5 there is the great thought of the trespass offering. When a trespass was done there were two matters: amends had to be made and a one fifth part added in compensation. Christ has made amends but He paid to God the one fifth part more and we enjoy this now. Thus, in Romans 5 we have the term 'much more' and the verb 'abound', vv. 15, 17, 20.

v. 1   **Therefore being justified by faith, we have peace with God through our Lord Jesus Christ:**

In verses 1-2 reference is made to our past guilt, present grace and future glory. Our past guilt has been taken account of in that we are justified; we have a present standing in divine grace and we rejoice in hope of the future glory of God.

The tense has the force of 'having been justified'. Justification is not a process: a person is completely justified at the moment of believing. We are '**justified**' which, negatively, involves acquittal from guilt and, positively, means that we have been declared just. This is '**through our Lord Jesus Christ**' and His work at Calvary. The only way to enjoy peace with God is to be justified by God and that by faith alone in our Lord Jesus Christ. The basis of justification is the blood of Calvary, v. 9, and its means is faith. This is not faith in an abstract way, such as faith in all God reveals or in Jesus' existence but is faith in His person and work. God is the 'justifier of him that believeth in Jesus' involving unqualified and unreserved trust in Jesus. This involves not just Calvary but the fact that He is exalted in heaven, His exaltation showing that His sacrifice has been accepted by God. Thus, in verse 2, '**by whom**', that is, by the risen man, we have access into this grace wherein we stand.

The result is that '**we have peace with God**'. Let us enter into its enjoyment. Our faith assures us of peace with God. Our sense of peace can lapse but peace itself cannot. This is not the peace of God but peace with God. This is the peace of knowing that whereas in my unconverted days I associated the judgement of God against my sins with the future, and that filled me with dread, this is no longer the case. I now associate the judgement of God against my sins with the past and I know that it is past forever. Thus, I have peace with God. We saw in chapter 4 the blessedness that God will not at all, in time or eternity, impute sin to the persons who trust Christ. This peace with God is as far as guilt is concerned and results in peace of conscience.

v. 2   **By whom also we have access by faith into this grace wherein we stand, and rejoice in hope of the glory of God.**

'**Access**' is not to be thought of just in terms of prayers. We have been freely admitted into this '**grace**' wherein we stand. We stand not only in divine righteousness but in the unmerited favour and acceptance of God. This is as true as our justification. In chapters 1-3 man is fallen: the words of Psalm 130 verse 3 are, 'If thou, Lord, shouldest mark iniquities, O Lord, who shall stand?' None would stand up to the examination of chapters 1-3 but now we have a standing in the grace of God. It is not a standing like a hired servant but like the prodigal clothed with the best robe, with ring on hand and shoes on feet. It is a standing in divine grace.

Further, 'we rejoice in hope' of future glory. Grace that has blotted out my guilty past and put me in a position of standing in favour with God now, makes me to hope, or exult, in hope of the glory of God. In chapter 3 every guilty mouth was stopped but now mouths are opened wide to joy in God.

The future 'glory of God' is God crowning with glory His own work of grace. 'Glory' in chapter 3 verse 23 is different. Here, it is not God's standard in view, as it is in chapter 3, nor His own glory, but the glory He bestows on those He has justified and who have a present standing in grace. Hebrews 2 tells us that He will bring many sons to glory and in Revelation 21 the city is described as having the glory of God. Indeed, the glory of God did lighten it. God will crown His work of grace by bestowing His glory on us.

v. 3   **And not only so, but we glory in tribulations also: knowing that tribulation worketh patience;**

We understand how we joy in hope of the glory of God but it is harder to understand how anyone can rejoice in tribulations. However, the apostle says, 'we joy in tribulations also'. At the end of chapter 8 he makes it plain that tribulation shall never separate us from the love of Christ. He is not teaching that we joy in tribulation for this reason: rather, we rejoice in tribulations for their effect in our experience and for what they produce.

'Tribulation worketh', or produces in us, endurance. James chapter 1 verse 3 says that 'the trial of your faith worketh patience'. This endurance is twofold. Firstly, when I am experiencing present trial and I wish it would be removed there is need of endurance. Then, if promised blessing is delayed there is need of endurance, 8. 25. Thus, if my trials are not speedily removed and the blessing I am longing for is being delayed I learn to submit without complaint to the will of God. This is easy to say; but it is the teaching of the verse.

Note that there is a full cycle of experience. In verse 2 we 'rejoice in hope of glory of God', a hope we received when we were saved. Now, in verse 3, 'we glory in tribulations also' and ultimately this produces hope, v. 4. The cycle therefore begins and ends with hope. Upon believing I had this hope of the glory of God and rejoiced in it but through my experiences down here the hope that was mine upon believing becomes more real to me.

v. 4   And patience, experience; and experience, hope:

'**Experience**' means proof as in 2 Corinthians chapter 2 verse 9, 'that I might know the proof of you' and Philippians chapter 2 verse 22, 'ye know the proof of' Timothy. My patience in tribulation is the experimental evidence of the proof of my faith. This is a very important matter. In Matthew chapter 13 verse 21 our Lord speaks of seed sown in rocky ground and then speaks of the time 'when tribulation cometh'. Tribulation detects the hypocrite but it is the proof of those with real faith. The hypocrite will collapse but the child of God will prosper. In the parable, the seed sown on rocky ground was withered by the sun. The sun produces growth in what is genuine but withers up what is not. Job says, 'Though he slay me, yet will I trust in him', Job 13. 15.

Experience produces '**hope**' and so the cycle is complete. In verse 2, hope is viewed objectively, being the result of my faith in Christ, but in verse 4 it is seen subjectively, produced by my experience. Verse 2 is hope received upon believing but verse 4 is that hope made real by experience. My endurance in tribulation does not cause my hope to waver, or grow dim, but makes it more real in my experience. This baffles the man of the world who thinks that a Christian in suffering will be driven further away from God and that he will think less of what God has given him, but the reverse is the case. Tribulation draws the child of God nearer to God and makes him to rejoice all the more and to think of the hope God gave him upon believing.

v. 5   And hope maketh not ashamed; because the love of God is shed abroad in our hearts by the Holy Ghost which is given unto us.

'**Hope maketh not ashamed**' in the sense that this hope will never be disappointed or cause me to be put to shame. These tribulations produce patience by my subjection to the will of God. This patience is a proof of my faith and produces in me subjectively the hope that faith has given me. This hope will never be disappointed nor will it ever put me to shame by reason of present tribulation. This is because there is added to me, as a child of God, the gracious work of the '**Holy Spirit**'. This is the first reference to the Holy Spirit in the epistle and we see in these verses that there is involved, as far as the believer is concerned, both the work and interest of the Godhead. It is wonderful to think that we are the objects of the work and interest of the Godhead: in verses 1-2, the work of Christ; in verse 5, the love of God; and, again in verse 5, the ministry of the Holy Spirit. There is here the work of Christ **for** me, the love of God **toward** me and the ministry of the Holy Spirit **in** me.

That which is **'shed abroad'** is not so much the person of the Holy Spirit but His work. God does not give His Spirit by measure. In 'shed abroad' there is the idea of rich and deep profusion. In John 7 our Lord speaks relative to the Holy Spirit in terms of rivers of living water flowing in abundance, John 7. 38. It is as Titus 3 where the apostle speaks of His being shed on us abundantly. The apostle here says that the Holy Spirit drenches my heart, to the point of overflowing, with a deep appreciation of God's love toward me. Whatever I pass through the hope is undimmed because I am in the present enjoyment of His love toward me as a guilty sinner. This is explained in the following verses.

v. 6   **For when we were yet without strength, in due
          time Christ died for the ungodly.**

The love of God was toward us despite our state. We were **'without strength'** and ungodly. 'Without strength' has in view the fact that we had no power to please God and keep His law: perhaps the Jew is particularly in the apostle's mind. As he speaks of the **'ungodly'**, perhaps he has the Gentiles in view. Not only did we have no strength, but also we had no desire after God. Despite this God set His own love upon us.

v. 7   **For scarcely for a righteous man will one die: yet
          peradventure for a good man some would even
          dare to die.**

God's love is superior to man's love at its best. **'Scarcely'**, in rare instances, would one die for a **'righteous man'**. Of course, Paul is not speaking forensically here but has in view those who are righteous in man's estimation. A **'good man'** describes one who is more than merely righteous. For such, some would dare, or venture, to die. Man will not sacrifice himself for an unworthy object but Christ did exactly that.

v. 8   **But God commendeth his love toward us, in that,**
             while we were yet sinners, Christ died for us.

In contrast to man's love at its best, God's love towards those who
were neither just nor good has already been '**commended**', or displayed. That love is not just to the just and good but to those who
were unworthy objects, those who were sinners.

v. 9   **Much more then, being now justified by his**
             blood, we shall be saved from wrath through him.

Five times in Romans 5 we read '**much more**', vv. 9, 10, 15, 17, 20.
Here, there is a contrast between His blood and Himself. Justification is by His blood but our future salvation is through Himself.
We have seen already that blood is the basis of justification for by
it every claim of divine justice was met. The one who shed His
blood is now alive in heaven and His being there at God's right
hand is the assurance of salvation from '**wrath**'. Every time that
wrath is mentioned in the New Testament it is connected with living men on earth. The sphere and subjects are always these. Thus,
this verse speaks of the wrath to come, not the Great White
Throne. We shall be '**saved**' through Himself. His coming will be
the occasion of that salvation. The apostle asks if the One who at
Calvary shed His blood to secure our justification would remain
unmoved in heaven if God poured out His wrath on earth. The
thought of His people passing through the Tribulation period is
therefore contrary to Scripture. Here, he speaks of the blood of
Christ and the person of Christ.

v. 10   **For if, when we were enemies, we were reconciled**
             to God by the death of his Son, much more, being
             reconciled, we shall be saved by his life.

In this verse there are another two contrasts, namely '**death**' and
'**life**'. The verse refers not to His life on earth but at God's right
hand. He said to His own, 'Because I live ye shall live also'.

In verse 9, it was His blood shed for our sins, with the result being
justification, but, in this verse, it is His death for our enmity,
with the result being reconciliation. His blood is Godward; His
death is manward in its character. His **blood** is propitiatory; His
death is substitutionary. These are important differences and it is
vital to note them. Reconciliation is always connected with His
death, see also Colossians chapter 1 and 2 Corinthians chapter 5.
Reconciliation has in view my distance in enmity. Death effects

reconciliation as it involves substitution. He took on Him all that was offensive to God about me and removed it from before God. It is the removal before God of the man my Saviour represented there at Calvary: there could be no reconciliation without the removal in death of the man who was at enmity with God.

It is always man being reconciled to God, not God to man. Reconciliation of man and man is mutual but this is not the case when man is reconciled to God. Justification has to do with sins whereas reconciliation is to do with the removal of myself as an enemy. Enemies are removed by death; sins are removed by blood. It should be carefully noted that in Colossians 1 the apostle speaks of the 'body of His flesh through death' and not just 'through death'. In the body of His flesh He took on Him everything about me that was offensive to God and in death it was removed. These are fine but very important distinctions.

We learn here that we are '**saved by his life**'. This does not refer to the future but to daily experience. The man who died to reconcile us now lives at God's right hand and secures our salvation day by day in life's experience. Everything is secured for us by the fact He lives for us in God's presence. Thus, Paul speaks of His death and His life and says that if God's Son was prepared to die for me, when an enemy, how much more is He prepared to live for me now that I am reconciled to God. At Calvary He died for me as an enemy; now He lives for me in heaven.

v. 11   **And not only so, but we also joy in God through our Lord Jesus Christ, by whom we have now received the atonement.**

This section finishes on a grand triumphant note. We '**joy in God**' and exult in Him. '**Atonement**' is really 'reconciliation' and stems from the previous verses. What a contrast this is to chapter 3 verse 19 where all mouths were stopped and all were guilty before God. Now our mouths are opened to exult in God. This is not rejoicing in blessings but in God Himself. All of the foregoing gives every reason why we should boast in God. In verse 6, we were without strength and, being ungodly, were without fear of God. In verse 8, we were sinners without holiness and, in verse 10, we were enemies, without love to God. Now, by divine grace, we enjoy peace. Our standing is in the grace of God; our rejoicing is in hope of the glory of God; our hearts are drenched in the love of God and therefore we boast in God Himself.

Chapter 5 verses 12-21 Federal Headship

At this point in the epistle Paul turns to speak not of individuals but of the whole race. He points to the results of Adam's transgression and God's grace for the human race. Up to now he has been speaking of 'sins' plural but now of 'sin': not now of sins committed but of sin as an evil principle. Verses 13-17 are in brackets, the purpose being to show the relationship of the law to sin: the apostle deals with the reason for the introduction of the law even though sin was already in the world before the law was introduced.

v. 12   **Wherefore, as by one man sin entered into the world, and death by sin; and so death passed upon all men, for that all have sinned:**

Here are two simple matters: sin entered and death passed. By one man sin entered and it passed on all, without exception. Paul thinks here of physical death rather than spiritual. Death is not the wages of 'sins' plural but of 'sin', the evil principle. Infants die not because of sins but because of sin. Thus, when God said to Adam, 'in the day thou eatest thereof in dying thou shalt die', Gen. 2. 17 literal, He spoke of physical death. The principle of death worked in Adam's body from the moment of sinning. Sin could not have entered without death also entering.

'**Wherefore**' is 'for this cause'. He has introduced the death of God's Son in verse 8 and goes on to point out another effect of His death but now in respect of a new race rather than individuals. Adam sinned as the head of the race. Some suggest that the last clause of the verse should read, 'all have sinned in Adam', and illustrate it by referring to Hebrews chapter 7. There, the writer states that when Abraham paid tithes to Melchisedec, Levi also paid tithes, as being in the loins of Abraham. This illustrates, they suggest, that the whole race was in the loins of Adam and accordingly sinned when he sinned. The King James Version is to be preferred here, however; the last clause is just an explanation of what has gone before. The statement is to prove the justice of the sentence rather than the fact that all sinned in Adam. Physical '**death**' is the result of sin and it passed upon '**all men**' without exception.

v. 13   **(For until the law sin was in the world: but sin is not imputed when there is no law.**

From here to verse 17 is a parenthesis dealing with sin and the law. The apostle meets a possible objection to verse 12 namely that if in that verse sin and death go back to Adam, why was there the necessity of the law?

The law entered between Adam and Christ but **'until the law'** there was sin in the world, as verse 12 indicates. God had to charge men with sin or He could not deal with them in death. Death is the wages of sin, not of transgression: prior to Sinai there was no transgression but there was sin. **'Sin is not imputed when there is no law'.** 'Imputed' is not as in chapter 4 verses 22-24 where it means to reckon judicially. Here the idea is putting fault to the personal account of anyone, as in Philemon verse 18, 'put that to my account'. Sin is not put down as a fault to a personal account when there is no law. Before Sinai man had not broken a stated law or a positive command.

The omission of the article before 'law' points to the principle of law introduced at Sinai.

v. 14   **Nevertheless death reigned from Adam to Moses, even over them that had not sinned after the similitude of Adam's transgression, who is the figure of him that was to come.**

'Nevertheless death reigned from Adam to Moses', as a monarch, because death is the wages of 'sin' rather than the wages of 'transgression'. Adam's sin was transgression in that he broke a stated law.

Adam is the **'figure'** or type of Him that was to come in terms of federal headship. Adam was the head of a fallen race: Christ is the head of a new race. Adam was not the head of the race until he sinned: he was not the head of the race in innocence. Clearly, he was the head of a fallen race only when he fell. Equally, Christ is not the federal head of the new race in virtue of His incarnation but in virtue of His death and resurrection.

v. 15   **But not as the offence, so also is the free gift. For if through the offence of one many be dead, much more the grace of God, and the gift by grace,**

which is by one man, Jesus Christ, hath abounded unto many.

From here to verse 17 there is a series of contrasts. In verse 15 there is a contrast in persons, in verse 16 of circumstances and in verse 17 of results.

Here, then, is a contrast in persons as the apostle deals with the recipients of salvation and the rejecters of salvation. Note that it is not 'all' but '**many**'. 'Many' in Scripture is never to do with offer, availability or direction but always to do with final analysis and ultimate classification. See the further comments regarding this in verses 18 and 19.

The contrast is made between the '**gift of grace**' and the issue of '**the offence**' of the one man. J. N. DARBY translates, 'But shall not the act of favour be as the offence?'. There is a contrast in character and transmission. Adam's offence was transmitted to the whole race so it is different from what comes from the death of Christ. Many died by the offence of one. The sentence of judgement was an absolute necessity, passed reluctantly; this was physical death. However, the gift of grace was not given reluctantly. If by the offence of the one man, Adam, the sentence of death was reluctantly passed on his race, the gift of grace by the one man, Christ, has abounded gladly and overwhelmingly to those who stand in connection with Him by faith. It is the free gift in grace, the gift of righteousness. It must be remembered that judgement is God's strange work.

v. 16 **And not as it was by one that sinned, so is the gift: for the judgment was by one to condemnation, but the free gift is of many offences unto justification.**

Here the emphasis is on a contrast in circumstances. The gift of righteousness comes in circumstances wholly dissimilar to those in which the judgement came. The '**judgment was by one to condemnation**': it was grounded on one single act. A literal translation might be, 'The judgement out of one to condemnation'. By contrast, the free gift was out of '**many offences**' to justification. God offers the free gift of righteousness despite our many offences. In that it says that it is by '**one that sinned**' and not by one that committed an offence, it embraces both those under law and not under it.

v. 17   For if by one man's offence death reigned by one;
         much more they which receive abundance of grace
         and of the gift of righteousness shall reign in life
         by one, Jesus Christ.)

Here the contrast is in results. Note the articles throughout: the
'one'. By reason of Adam's 'offence' death reigns as a monarch:
men live under its authority. However, they who receive the
'abundance of grace' by faith, and the 'gift of righteousness',
shall reign in the future with, 'by' or 'because of', Christ in the
enjoyment of eternal life.

v. 18   Therefore as by the offence of one judgment came
         upon all men to condemnation; even so by the
         righteousness of one the free gift came upon all
         men unto justification of life.

The parenthesis is now closed and the apostle reverts to the argument he commenced in verse 12.

Notice the phrases, 'judgment came' and 'the free gift came'.
J. N. DARBY translates, 'So then as it was by one offence toward all
to condemnation so by one righteousness toward all men for justification of life'. We note, firstly, 'one offence', of Adam, toward all
men and, secondly, 'one righteousness' toward all men for justification of life. It is important to note the preposition. The word
'upon' (eis) is really 'unto' or 'towards'. It was not 'upon' all men,
for Adam's offence did not bring condemnation on all men without hope but it brought condemnation toward all men in terms of
its scope and direction. Thus, by Adam's one offence all are threatened by condemnation: it is 'towards' them in its direction, not
'upon' them in its final state. Therefore, Paul uses the word 'all'.

Judgement is present but 'condemnation' is future and eternal.
The sentence is passed in time but it is executed in eternity; it is the
second death. Thus, all men are threatened with eternal death by
Adam's sin. In verse 12 death passed on all men: in verse 18 condemnation is toward all men. All may physically die but not all
will be eternally condemned.

In the second half of the verse the word 'upon' (eis) is again 'unto',
or 'towards'. This justification is not 'upon' all men but it is 'towards' all men in terms of its direction. 'One righteousness' is not
a simple righteous act but the accomplished righteousness of Calvary which is, of course, 'towards', rather than 'upon', all. It was

not the character of the act that brought life but the accomplishment of the act. Righteousness was procured for us in His one act at Calvary. Therefore, we must distinguish between the act and its accomplishment. The accomplishment is the result of the act. It is what is accomplished and becomes available that is in view; the phrase is not a comment on the righteousness of the one who accomplished it. It is here an accomplished righteousness. Our Saviour accomplished it by His death at Calvary. In the verse there is more than a comparison brought before us. It is rather a contrast between one offence and one accomplished righteousness: this is something more than a simple act.

'**Justification of life**' is life on a righteous basis; that is, a righteous title to eternal life. It is not practical, righteous Christian living that is in view.

v. 19   **For as by one man's disobedience many were made sinners, so by the obedience of one shall many be made righteous.**

It is important to note the change of language. In verse 12 it is 'one . . . and all men'. In verse 18 it is the same, again speaking of 'one' and 'all men'. In verse 19, however, it is different: the apostle speaks of 'one' and 'many'. J. N. DARBY translates, 'For as indeed by the disobedience of the one man the many have been constituted sinners, so also by the obedience of the one the many will be constituted righteous'. '**The many**' are those who refuse the proffered righteousness. They are '**sinners**' for ever. Whenever the word is 'many' it is never used in terms of the offer, or availability, but always in terms of final result or ultimate classification. Thus, in terms of the final analysis many will be constituted sinners eternally. Sinners they are and sinners they will remain as they refused proffered grace.

'**By the obedience of one**', or by the one act of obedience when He handed Himself over to the judgement of God, the many will be constituted '**righteous**'. Note that it is not 'all', for that would result in universalism, but '**the many**'. These are they who accept God's offered righteousness as the gift of grace. It would be as wrong to say that Adam's disobedience affected the many as it would be to say that the value of the death of Christ is only available for the many. The final analysis is that many are constituted sinners eternally and many are constituted righteous for ever. So 'all' is used in terms of direction and availability and 'many' in terms of ultimate classification. The apostle is not so much dealing here with the means of salvation but with ultimate classification.

Christ's personal obedience in His life could never procure righteousness for us: it was the accomplishment of what He did at Calvary, a particular act of obedience, which brings salvation.

v. 20   **Moreover the law entered, that the offence might abound. But where sin abounded, grace did much more abound:**

'**Moreover**' is 'but'. In referring to '**law**' entering it should be noted that there is no article. The apostle is referring to the principle of law keeping which came in by Moses. In verse 12, speaking of the fact that sin entered, the word used is 'came', but when it is stated here that the law '**entered**' a different word is employed. It means 'to come in beside or along with', that is, in addition to sin. The definite article being omitted it reads, '**that offence might abound**'. It is not that 'sin' might abound for if God brought in the law to make sin abound God would be made the author of sin. This is not true, of course. In saying that the 'offence' might abound Paul means that the law came in alongside sin that sin might be seen in its character as an offence against God. The word '**abound**' indicates that the law was not added just that offence might abound; God did not give it with a view to the offence abounding but that was the result. Such is the human heart that it rebels against commands.

Then the apostle says '**where sin abounded**', not where the offence abounded. If it was by the giving of the law that sin was seen as an offence then to use the word 'offence' here would suggest that grace is limited to those under the law. Rather, he speaks in a wider sphere to all humanity.

v. 21   **That as sin hath reigned unto death, even so might grace reign through righteousness unto eternal life by Jesus Christ our Lord.**

'**Sin**' today reigns in the power of death. However, the result of the death of Christ is that '**grace**' reigning through righteousness unto eternal life. God's answer to sin reigning is '**eternal life**' and thus grace reigning '**through righteousness**' is the character of the gospel in the present day.

Chapter 6 verses 1-23 The Believer and Sin

This chapter divides into two sections. In both verses 1 and 15 the question is asked, 'What then?' In verse 1, 'Shall we continue in sin?' In verse 15, 'Shall we sin?' The question of verse 1 is answered in verses 2-14. We have been delivered from the dominion of sin by having died to sin with Christ. In this section the emphasis is on reckoning, v. 11. The second question is answered in verses 16-23. The apostle says that we have changed masters. We were servants of sin but are now the servants of righteousness. Here, the emphasis is not on reckoning but on a person's will and motive, see verses 16 and 19. To 'yield' involves the will.

In chapter 6 Paul anticipates the complaint of the moralists that the doctrine of grace gives liberty to sin. They would object that if grace alone, apart from works, saves from the penal consequences of sin we may continue to sin. In chapter 5 verses 12-21 the doctrine of grace has been expounded. There, grace has abounded in verses 15, 17, and 20. Shall we take advantage of the super abounding grace of God and continue in sin? 'Far be the thought!' JND.

Paul deals with the matter in a different manner from John in his First Epistle. In 1 John 3, John says that to commit sin habitually is a denial of the new birth. In Romans, however, Paul brings to bear upon the Christian walk the death and resurrection of Christ. Up to chapter 5 he speaks of His death and resurrection as it relates to our need as sinners, cf. 4. 25, but now of His death and resurrection as it relates to our walk as Christians. The teaching is that by His death my old life has been brought to an end but by His resurrection a new life has been opened up to me.

Before salvation we lived in sin, v. 2, and we served sin, v. 6. In chapter 6, sin is seen as a life, v. 1; a master, v. 6; a monarch, v. 12; and a principle, v. 13. We were not only surrounded by it but we were also under its dominion. This should not, of course, characterise us now. In verse 2, we have died to sin: in verse 6, our old man has been crucified so that we cannot serve sin. Thus, we observe that a distinction is made between our having died and our old man having been crucified. We ourselves died, but the old man was crucified.

In **verses 1-7**, we have died to sin in a three-fold way. Firstly, we died two thousand years ago when Christ died. Then, when we trusted Him as guilty sinners, we accepted this great fact by faith. Lastly, in baptism we made a public profession of it. The subject of the verses is sin, so the emphasis is on death and burial. There is deliverance from sin reigning in our lives only by our reckoning we are dead and buried. We are baptised unto Jesus Christ in verse 3, but also we are baptised unto His death. The expressions buried, v. 4, planted together, v. 5, and crucified, v. 6, help us to understand that in the divine reckoning we have been placed in the sphere of death and there we must remain. We are to reckon ourselves to be in the place of death in order to have deliverance from sin. As far as sin is concerned, we are to remain buried in death.

There is, however, a positive side to this truth. If, in verse 2, we do not live in sin, in verse 4 we walk in newness of life. This is a lovely expression. Then, if in verse 6 we do not serve sin, in verse 11 we live unto God. This ought to characterise us day by day.

In **verses 8-14** we have not just died to sin but we have died with Christ. However, we must notice that in verse 8 we are assured of future life with Him, 'we shall live with him', and in verse 11 we are, in the meantime, 'alive in him'. This is something we believe rather than something we are to reckon. As to the future, it is a trust; we believe that we shall live with Him. As to the present, we are alive in Him. In verse 10, Christ, having died to the world where sin rules, now lives unto God. What He did in this world of sin when He was here, He is now doing at God's right hand and we are living in Him. Because of this, we live to God, as He lives to God.

v. 1   **What shall we say then? Shall we continue in sin, that grace may abound?**

'**What shall we say then?**' occurs often in Romans. The apostle employs the deliberative subjunctive when he asks, '**Shall we continue in sin?**' He is speaking not just of mere continuance in sin but of persevering in it in will and act. The same idea is expressed where Paul says to Timothy, 'Take heed unto thyself, and unto the doctrine; continue in them', 1 Tim. 4. 16. By grace, the believer is eternally secure but this should not make us careless in respect of our daily lives. To be careless as to sin raises a question mark over salvation. This is true of every Christian. Thus, John says 'if we sin', not 'when we sin', 1 John 2. 1. 'If' allows for the possibility; 'when' implies habit. No child of God can persevere in sin.

v. 2　　　God forbid. How shall we, that are dead to sin, live any longer therein?

'God forbid' is simply 'perish the thought'. To continue in sin is not worthy of consideration. The apostle does not approach the question of continuing in sin with reference to it being heinous, or from the standpoint of God's character, or of grieving God's Son but rather from the standpoint that to continue in sin is a contradiction of what is true of every Christian, whether or not it is realised. It is not that we should die to sin but that we 'have died to sin'. It is not 'we have died' as if some have and some have not, but this is true of every Christian. In Romans 6 it is essential to see that it is not Christ's death for me or for my sins that is in view but my death with Christ. It is not my crimes being blotted out but me, the criminal, being put away. Further, this is not spiritual death, which is death 'in sin'. That is a state where a person is devoid of any living principle Godward and is death as far as God is concerned. Here, it is dead 'to sin' as governing my life. Being dead 'in sin' is being dead to what is right but here Paul speaks of being dead to what is wrong.

If we died to sin, how can we 'live any longer' in it? We lived in sin actually and morally but since every Christian has died to sin legally from the standpoint of God we can no longer live actually in it, surrounded by it, our bodies enveloped in it, sin being the sinners' vital air.

v. 3　　　Know ye not, that so many of us as were baptized into Jesus Christ were baptized into his death?

The word 'buried' indicates that the apostle is speaking about water baptism. This does not save the soul or make one fit for heaven; rather, it is to do with living here on earth. Baptism is upon confession that He died for me and that I died with Him. Some might wonder if 'so many of us' implies that some were not baptised but the Greek has no such thought. All who were saved on and after the day of Pentecost were baptised. The phrase is simply an emphatic expression for 'everyone'.

Baptism is into (eis), or unto, Jesus Christ. This is not baptism in the Spirit, therefore, as baptism does not give a person a place in Christ. The context always determines which baptism is in view. Both times here it is 'unto' as 1 Corinthians chapter 10 verse 2 where the fathers were baptised 'unto' Moses. They were not baptised 'into' Moses. Baptism is therefore a declaration that we belong to Him, that we obey Him and that we accept His leadership. In 1 Corinthians 10 Israel were in the desert where they had never been and were shut up to their leader Moses; in our baptism we say we belong to Jesus Christ and will obey Him, our leader. Thus, there is to be no self-pleasing or self-will.

The above is positive but there is a negative side to the truth also. We have been '**baptised unto his death**'. As far as sin is concerned we are to remain in the place of death, neither responding to it nor answering its appeal. When people are saved and trying to be holy they often look inward and try to die to self, something which cannot be done. We are in fact to look backward to Calvary and realise we are dead. James says we are to resist the devil and he will flee from us but the same verse says we are to submit to God and in God's strength resist. We do not resist sin, however, for we have died to it. This is never to do with feeling dead but accepting by faith that it is true. Also, it is not just that we are to believe this truth but to reckon that what God says is true and by God's grace to make it true in our lives. Sin never dies, nor the law, but we die to it.

v. 4   **Therefore we are buried with him by baptism into death: that like as Christ was raised up from the dead by the glory of the Father, even so we also should walk in newness of life.**

'**Baptism unto death**' is the reverse of the natural order in which death is followed by burial. Here, however, we are buried unto death. We are buried by means of baptism, not by the mere act but by what it symbolises. We have testified in our baptism that we have been laid in the same grave as our Saviour and that we are in the place of death as far as sin is concerned. A salvation which does not change the life will not take to heaven. The baptism of a believer is a very solemn occasion. After all, a burial is not an entertainment; it is a solemn declaration.

Baptism is not merely a confession of salvation. It is a public declaration that we have died to sin and that therefore sin is no longer the ruling principle in our life. This is not to do with battling with sin, for none is equal to it; nor is it to do with gaining victory over sin; rather, it is the matter of deliverance from it by recognising we have died to it. We are laid in the same grave as our Saviour. We confess that there is no hope in self and thus baptism is not our sins being swept away, but ourselves. The result is that we cannot now serve sin.

As long as Christ's sacred body lay in the tomb the Father's glory was at stake but **'the glory of the Father'** raised from the dead the One who is His Son. It is after this standing that the Christian walks **'in newness of life'** where the governing principle is the glory of the Father. Thus, that life is new in kind and course. It is linked with the resurrection of Christ and this is the significance of the words **'that like as'**. Just as Christ's death is brought before us in a unique way in Romans 6, so is His resurrection. In this chapter He is not raised for our justification, or by the power of God, as in Ephesians 1, but a unique expression is employed, 'by the glory of the Father'. The Father's glory raised His Son from the dead into a resurrection sphere; a sphere above the world of sin and shame. The believer now lives above the plane of sin and shame in a resurrection sphere, never to go back to the former sin and shame of unconverted days, controlled and governed by the glory of the Father. This means the governing principle is not, 'there is no harm in this or that' as is the case with the unregenerate man. Now, the governing principle is, 'what glory is there for the Father in this?'

In Ephesians 1 the power of God raised Him (Christ) as it has also raised me; this is to do with conversion. Here, however, it is to do with the character of our lives now as a Christian in the world. His glory demanded His resurrection; His power performed it. Thus, the glory of the Father now makes demands upon us. We will not find it easy both because of the world and the low standards of the vast majority of Christians. But let us set our sights high and live for the glory of the Father! This would revolutionise our lives if we lived by it. Take courage, and no matter the cost and sacrifice put everything to that test.

We should ask ourselves as to whether we are living true to our baptism. The practicality can often be so different from the theology. The more we walk in newness of life the more the negative side takes care of itself. Believing is once for all with continuing effect but reckoning it as true is a daily experience. We cannot do this in our own strength so, in chapter 8, we are to put the doctrine into effect by the power of the indwelling Spirit. In that chapter, the body is dead because of sin but the spirit is life because of righteousness.

In Colossians chapter 2 verse 11 Paul speaks of having 'put off the body of the sins of the flesh'. This is virtually the same truth as here. In the Old Testament circumcision dealt with one member of the body but in the New Testament spiritual circumcision is in respect of the whole body. In Romans we have died to sin; in Colossians we have died to the world. In respect of sin the apostle emphasises death and burial; in respect of the world he emphasises burial and resurrection, cf. Col. 2. 12. In Romans the emphasis is on deliverance from sin by death; in Colossians we live a resurrection life above the level of the world. Romans 6 is the Red Sea; Colossians 2 is the Jordan. We never read of Israel coming out of the Red Sea, 'in the midst of the sea' is the expression which is used. With the Jordan, however, the emphasis is on their coming out, the expression being 'clean passed through', with stones on the other side to prove it. Thus, in Romans 6 we are in the Red Sea whereas in Colossians 2 we are above the level of the world in the land.

Submergence and emergence is the meaning of 'baptism'. In Romans 6 the emphasis is on 'submergence', death, with emergence being there by implication. In Colossians the emphasis is on emergence, resurrection, with burial being there by implication. Baptism is submergence and emergence with different aspects being emphasised in the different passages.

v. 5   **For if we have been planted together in the likeness of his death, we shall be also in the likeness of his resurrection:**

'**Planted together**' conveys the idea of being identified with Him in the likeness, or similitude of His death, resembling His death. It is important to note the italicised words in the phrase '**we shall be also** *in the likeness* **of his resurrection**'. The apostle is not thinking of the likeness of His resurrection in coming out of baptismal waters but actually speaks of our resurrection at His coming. As long as we are here we are in a world of sin where sin is ruling. We are to keep ourselves in the place of death until the moment comes when we will be delivered out of it at His coming. There will only be full and final deliverance from sin when He comes again.

v. 6   **Knowing this, that our old man is crucified with
him, that the body of sin might be destroyed, that
henceforth we should not serve sin.**

'**Knowing**' refers to doctrine based on facts in the past. The term
'**old man**' is used in a corporate sense and refers to the whole race
in its Adam standing. This was '**crucified with**' Christ at Calvary.
It was there that the end of all flesh came before God. A judicial
sentence was passed by God on the whole race and man in
his Adamic standing was terminated at Calvary. As far as I am
concerned individually this relates to the old nature I have as
belonging to that old Adamic race, but the teaching here is that the
whole Adamic race was crucified with Christ.

The '**body of sin**' is this mortal body which is not destroyed but
annulled, or rendered powerless to sin. Verse 12 explains 'body of
sin'. It is our mortal body which provides the territory where sin
can reign. It has been 'annulled', a word that is also used in
Hebrews where the writer states that our Saviour, by His death,
'destroyed' him that had the power of death, 2. 14. The idea is not
so much that the devil has been destroyed but his power in relation to death has been annulled. The purpose in view is that
'**henceforth**' we should not be slaves to sin. The old man is root;
the body of sin is the fruit. The old man relates to a sinful nature;
the body of sin is where that nature expresses itself.

In summary, the old man was crucified and the body of sin is
annulled. As we have observed, this mortal body provided the
monarch, sin, with the territory in which to reign and to exercise
its mastery. Sin made its pressing and relentless demands on the
members of our bodies with the result that the members of our
bodies became sin's weapons to do what is not right, cf. v. 13. Now
the service of sin has been brought to an end; our old man has
been crucified. The whole Adamic race corporately was crucified.
There are important distinctions to make. Our old man did not
die; I died. Death is natural; crucifixion is judicial. People may die
through such things as disease, old age, or accident but crucifixion
is a sentence of judgement. It was done deliberately by one person
to another and, in the case of our Lord, Pilate passed sentence and
the soldiers carried it out. Here, God passed sentence on the
whole of Adam's race and that sentence was executed on our
Saviour at Calvary. There the end of all flesh came before God
because there was nothing in it that could please God. It could

only produce evil. Thus, the old man, which in us is the nature we have by being a child of Adam and which the law could not calm, had to be crucified. God has condemned it, with this in view that the body be powerless to sin.

v. 7   **For he that is dead is freed from sin.**

'**He that has died is freed from sin**' or 'justified' from sin. This is a legal word. A person who dies is freed from his master's jurisdiction. Sin has no dominion over a dead person. We have died to sin and are not sin's subjects any longer. In that sense sin has no more jurisdiction over us. Note carefully that throughout the apostle speaks of sin, not sins. Sin, as a master, makes its relentless demands but through death we are free from its principle.

vv. 8-9   **Now if we be dead with Christ, we believe that we shall also live with him: Knowing that Christ being raised from the dead dieth no more; death hath no more dominion over him.**

We are dead with Him now, having died at Calvary with Him but we shall live with Him in the future. In view of this glorious prospect of being in the sphere unsullied by sin, we should accept now that as far as sin is concerned we are dead to it. We cannot live for both worlds; therefore we must live for Him now and not yield to the demands of sin.

To '**believe**' is to trust and is connected not to the past but to the future. We believe we shall live with Him when the whole life of the redeemed body is one continuous and uninterrupted outflow to God in a scene where there will be nothing about us to tempt us, and nothing within to yield. '**Reckon**', v. 11, is connected with the present. It is more than 'knowing', vv. 6 and 9, and believing. It is accepting the fact as true and acting in the light of it.

v. 10   **For in that he died, he died unto sin once: but in that he liveth, he liveth unto God.**

Christ '**died**' to the world in which '**sin**' now rules. He is now '**living unto God**', something as true in His humiliation here as is now true in heaven. Every moment was lived unto God, doing the Father's will. Since He is our life and we are alive in Him, we too must live unto God. This is high ground and is to be worked out in practise by the 'reckoning' of verse 11, which involves the will.

This is also so in verses 12-13, where the apostle says 'let not' and 'yield', our attention is directed to exercise of the will.

v. 11   **Likewise reckon ye also yourselves to be dead indeed unto sin, but alive unto God through Jesus Christ our Lord.**

The truth the apostle has been declaring is that we are dead to sin. God says it is actually true and we are to act accordingly. Thus, when the sin of our former life makes its appeal we are to '**reckon**', to count it as true, that we have died to it and thereby disallow its appeal. We are also to reckon in a positive way that we are alive unto God '**through** (*en*) **Christ Jesus**'.

The change in language is to be noted. In verse 6, our old man was crucified 'with' Him. In verse 8, Paul states that we have died 'with' Him and shall also live 'with' Him. 'With' clearly has the thought of identification but in this verse, 'in' Christ Jesus, it is different. 'In' does not just express a positional truth but speaks of a living union with Him. We are, then, not simply 'alive to God' but 'alive to God in Christ Jesus'. Because there is this union in life in Christ Jesus there is the power to live unto God. In verse 10, our Saviour, in God's presence, lives unto God; what He did down here He now does in heaven. We are alive in Him and, by reason of this union we have with Him, we also live to God. We live in Him to God.

v. 12   **Let not sin therefore reign in your mortal body, that ye should obey it in the lusts thereof.**

In verses 12-13 the apostle speaks of the practical outworking of reckoning ourselves dead to sin and alive to God. Observe how one's will is involved. Paul speaks negatively in verse 12, 'let not', and positively in verse 13, 'yield'.

From a negative standpoint, Paul says, '**let not sin reign**'. In effect, he says do not give sin a foothold on the first step to the throne of your heart. We are not to parley or fight with it for we are no match for this monarch. Rather, we are to accept we have died to it and seek divine help not to respond or obey. The '**mortal body**' is just the territory that sin desires and it is there that sin produces lust and evil desires, cf. Jas. 1. 14-15. Sin wants to reign in the life of every believer without exception. We are to see that sin does not reign in our mortal bodies.

v. 13   Neither yield ye your members as instruments of
          unrighteousness unto sin: but yield yourselves
          unto God, as those that are alive from the dead,
          and your members as instruments of
          righteousness unto God.

Now, from the positive standpoint, we are to 'yield'. The demands
of sin on the members of the body are always to do what is not
right. Thus, the apostle says we are not to yield our members as
instruments, or weapons, of unrighteousness. Do not yield to sin;
rather, yield to God. The first use of the verb is in the present tense;
do not keep yielding your members to sin. The second time the
verb is used it is in the aorist: this is the critical resolve of all who
are saved. This happens ideally at conversion; then there is the
continual yielding of the members, for the body is the vehicle for
accomplishing God's will and for the expression of minds and
hearts which are yielded to Him.

In Romans chapters 1 and 16 the apostle speaks of the 'obedience
of faith'. Faith that saves is faith that obeys. This is what is in view
in Acts chapter 16 verse 30, 'What must I do to be saved?', and
Acts chapter 9 verse 6, 'Lord what wilt thou have me to do?'. This
is faith's obedience which becomes characteristic of Christian living. We will never reach sinless perfection here; we do not have
complete victory over sin. Out of the heart, the seat of thinking,
there proceed adulteries and many other evils. These do not start
in the body but in the heart. The secret in all of this is setting the
mind on things above. Read Scripture and have some verses in
your mind to think about in your spare moments. If the eye is single the whole body is full of light. Have a single eye for Christ.

We are alive to God in Christ Jesus so we are to yield as being
alive. As having died to sin and sin finding no response in us, and
as being alive to God, let us yield ourselves entirely to God. God
never calls us to surrender anything grudgingly. Here, it is not
the surrender which is the last resort of an enemy to his captor. To
yield is to 'present worshipfully'. It is easy, as a Christian, to carry
out the will of God grudgingly rather than 'doing the will of God
from the heart', Eph. 6. 6. No one is sufficient in themselves to be
their own master. It is a question of yielding either to sin or to
God. One or other will be master. Let us not allow the members of
our bodies to be instruments, or weapons, for doing what is not

right. The unregenerate do that but the believer is to be yielded to God.

The order in the verse is very important. It is firstly '**yield yourselves**' and then '**your members**'. This is the order for practical Christian living. The reason so many fail is that we start with the members of our body first. What is involved here is that we say to God, 'Take my hands, my feet, my eyes, and my intellect: let them all be Thine and only Thine and always Thine'. This is Christian living.

v. 14   **For sin shall not have dominion over you: for ye are not under the law, but under grace.**

'**Under law**' man was under sin's '**dominion**'. Note the effect of the law in such verses as: 'by the law is the knowledge of sin', 3. 20; 'the law entered, that the offence might abound', 5. 20; and 'I had not known sin, but by the law', 7. 7. The law exposes man's evil nature. Then, we learn that the mind of the flesh is not subject to the law of God and that it is impossible for it to be so, 8. 7. The prohibitions of the law only serve to stir up hostility to God in the flesh. '**Under grace**', however, it is different. We are alive to God in Christ Jesus. As we have already seen, we are not simply 'alive to God' but 'alive to God in Christ Jesus'. There is the power to live unto God because there is this union in life in Christ Jesus. Thus, 'sin shall not have dominion over you: for ye are not under law, but under grace'.

Before salvation, we turned a blind eye to gospel verses, and a deaf ear to gospel preaching, yielding the members of our body instead to that which was not right. Then, we would revel in what would stir up evil emotions and those things that would check the conviction of the Holy Spirit. Now this is no longer to characterise us; yield your members to God in the power of the Holy Spirit, upon which the apostle enlarges in chapter 8.

Thus, the question of verse 1, 'What shall we say then? Shall we continue in sin, that grace may abound?' is answered. Sin shall not have dominion over you; it would if you were under the law but not now that you are under grace.

In **verses 15-23** there is a change of subject. In verses 1-14 the question of verse 1 is answered by the fact of God's judgements on the old man and the deliverance of the Christian by his association with the death and resurrection of Christ. The question of verse 15 is answered by an appeal to motives. Paul argues that having been set free according to the liberty of grace I must not use this liberty as a licence for sinning. As the power of sin is the law so grace is the power for holiness.

v. 15   **What then? shall we sin, because we are not under the law, but under grace? God forbid.**

The doctrine of grace assures us of exemption from the penal consequences of sin but no one saved by grace can ever live carelessly. We have seen that we cannot continue in sin as having died to it. Now, we do not commit sin because it is wholly inconsistent with a profession of change of masters. This is the theme of the section. We have changed masters. To obey a master, sin, from whose mastery I have been delivered, would be an abuse of divine grace.

v. 16   **Know ye not, that to whom ye yield yourselves servants to obey, his servants ye are to whom ye obey; whether of sin unto death, or of obedience unto righteousness?**

'**Know ye not**' indicates that what is about to be said should be self-evident. He speaks of the will again when he uses the word '**yield**' and personifies '**sin**' and '**obedience**'. The apostle establishes that bond service, once accepted, is binding and forbids divided servitude. If one freely yields to a master, it is the master of personal choice. If I yielded to sin in unconverted days it resulted in death but yielding to obedience in conversion issues in practical righteousness. Verse 17 shows that the yielding to obedience is at conversion. Christian righteousness is not doing something simply because it is right, because a man of the world may do this. It is possible to do a right thing out of pride but Christians are bond-slaves of obedience. We do right because it is God's will.

v. 17   **But God be thanked, that ye were the servants of sin, but ye have obeyed from the heart that form of doctrine which was delivered you.**

We were '**the servants of sin**' but obeyed at the time of conversion. This obedience was '**from the heart**' for it was neither grudging nor reluctant. Initial obedience to '**that form of doctrine**' moulded their lives. The word 'form' is translated in chapter 5 verse 14 as 'type'. It is sometimes used of persons, 'ye have us for an ensample', Phil. 3. 17, or incidents, 'now all these things happened unto them for ensamples', 1 Cor. 10. 11. Perhaps the thought is of 'that into which you were delivered and that now moulds your life'. This was the apostolic doctrine. Some liken this to molten metal taking shape from the mould, of being molten by the power of God to run into the apostolic mould. Others say Paul still continues the metaphor of slavery and has in mind being taken out of the hands of one master and put into the hands of another. The ruling principle of the gospel is obedience. There is, therefore, no room for self-will or self-pleasing; obedience is not optional in Christianity. The apostle began his Christian life by asking, 'What must I do?'. It is good to begin each day in the same way. Sadly, so many profess salvation with no change in the life.

v. 18   **Being then made free from sin, ye became the servants of righteousness.**

'**Being then made free from sin**' is 'having got your freedom from sin'. This is obtained through obedience to another. No man is sufficient for himself. If we try to be our own master we are brought under Satan's power. At conversion we obtained freedom from sin and became 'enslaved' '**to righteousness**'. This is not slavery to the righteous requirements of the law but rather righteousness becomes the established rule of life. Having capitulated to grace we ought to do only that which is right.

v. 19   **I speak after the manner of men because of the infirmity of your flesh: for as ye have yielded your members servants to uncleanness and to iniquity unto iniquity; even so now yield your members servants to righteousness unto holiness.**

When Paul says, 'I speak humanly on account of the weakness of your flesh' JND, he refers to the preceding teaching regarding slavery. After all, slavery is Christianity at its lowest level: at its highest level it is the compulsion of love. The Romans were still in the '**flesh**', that which opposes the spirit. Before conversion their will was exercised in yielding as bond-slaves to '**uncleanness**', unto lawlessness. They were bond-slaves to a craving for that which was evil and to '**lawlessness**' and even greater lawlessness. There was an increasing opposition to any restraint of God. Now, however, they '**yield**' to righteousness. Notice this distinction, that in verse 18 it is 'servants of righteousness' whereas in verse 19 it is 'servants to righteousness'. They are now bondslaves to do only that which is right with '**holiness**' being the end in view.

Note, therefore, that it is not unto increased righteousness but holiness, or sanctification, the moral purity of one's life.

v. 20   **For when ye were the servants of sin, ye were free from righteousness.**

This is an unusual statement. Once, the apostle says, you were, without doubt, not the bondservants of righteousness; in respect of **'righteousness'** you were **'free'**, not being concerned about it. Paul is being ironic, as the unconverted boast in their freedom. There was no freedom before conversion as they were 'slaves of sin'.

v. 21   **What fruit had ye then in those things whereof ye are now ashamed? for the end of those things is death.**

'**Then'** and '**now'** marks the change of conversion. In things of which they were '**now ashamed'** there was no '**fruit'**, no profit, peace or happiness. It ought to be noted that they were ashamed of their former lives; no doubt they did not parade the sins of those lives in testimony meetings. After all, '**the end of those things is death'**, not spiritual death, as they were already spiritually dead, and not eternal death, which is the eternal continuation of spiritual death. Paul says that the former life gives shame now and its end is physical death. The fruit of their lives was corrupt; it only sufficed for time and its end was death.

v. 22   **But now being made free from sin, and become servants to God, ye have your fruit unto holiness, and the end everlasting life.**

'But now, having got your freedom from sin' JND, something they had now obtained, they became '**servants to God'**, the real master of the justified. It is not just as before, being servants of obedience, servants to righteousness, and servants to the rule of doctrine. They were now bondservants to the real Master to whom complete subjection is owed, to God Himself.

Now, they have fruit unto sanctification. '**Ye have'** is emphatic: you have your fruit now, '**unto sanctification'**, which is being set apart to God in daily life. '**Everlasting life'** is something we have as a present possession but here the future is in view in which we shall have everlasting life in full and unfettered enjoyment. In verse 21, we have the past, in verse 22, both the present and the future.

v. 23   **For the wages of sin is death; but the gift of God is eternal life through Jesus Christ our Lord.**

We should note that 'weapons' in verse 13 is a military expression, as is '**wages**'. John the Baptist said to the soldiers, 'Be content with your wages', Luke 3. 14.

The '**death**' of which the apostle speaks is temporal; it is physical death. It is not spiritual, which is true now of the unbeliever, neither is it eternal death, for that is not the wages of sin but of sins. Death is the wages of sin; eternal death is the wages of sins. Sentence will be passed on all according to their sins. Thus, here it is physical death. Sin is not the nature we have but is the evil principle that operates upon the evil nature we possess as having come from a fallen race. Sin is the principle which entered into the world consequent on Adam's sin in the garden. This evil principle still remains and death is its inevitable consequence.

However, '**the gift of God**', the 'act of favour of God' JND, is '**eternal life**'. Life is not just ceaseless duration but there is in view all it brings in eternity. We are all subject to the wages of sin but we have a gift that eclipses these wages by far. If death is the wages of sin we would have expected that eternal life is the issue of holiness but this is not so. Salvation is a gift altogether apart from human merit or effort. Sin is the procuring cause of death but sanctification is not the procuring cause of eternal life; it is but the training for the enjoyment of what is essentially a gift of divine grace and this is enjoyed '**in Christ Jesus our Lord**'. Eternal life was manifested in our Saviour in His incarnation and life, 1 John 1. 1-4. It was procured for us at Calvary, Rom. 5. 18-21. Eternal life here has not so much been procured for us 'through' Him but is secured for us 'in' (*en*) Him. Eternal life is found only twice in the Old Testament, in Daniel 12 and Psalm 133. The promise of eternal life in the Old Testament was connected with earth and the enjoyment of endless life on earth under the reign of God through Christ. What we have now, however, is in Christ Jesus our Lord and it really belongs to heaven. It was procured in His death and is secured in Him as a risen Man in glory.

Chapter 7 verses 1-25 The Believer and the Law
In this chapter the apostle deals with the believer and God's law. We read twice in chapter 6, 'Ye are not under law but under grace'. In chapter 6 we are **freed from sin**, vv. 7, 18 and 22. We have seen that this is true of each child of God. The metaphor is slavery; we have been freed from one master to serve another. In chapter 7 we are **freed from the law**. The metaphor is marriage; we have been freed from one husband to be married to another. In each case we have been delivered by death. It is not that sin or the law dies but we die to them.

The law was given 'that the offence might abound', 5. 20, that man might appreciate he has a rebellious nature which the law incites and which makes man antagonistic. The law was not given to make men sinners for we are that by birth as children of Adam's race. Also, the law was not given to make men sin, for men could then blame God. God is never the author of sin. Man needs deliverance from law and sin. This chapter does not deal with deliverance from the curse of a broken law; that was effected by Christ's death for me, Gal. 3. 13. Rather, it deals with deliverance from law keeping as the principle by which a man might live and with the removal of the law breaker by death.

The chapter may be divided in a variety of ways. In verses 1-6, the apostle speaks of the believer generally and of that which is true of every believer. Note the words 'ye also', v. 4, 'we', v. 5, and 'we', v. 6. Then, in verses 7-13, he speaks of the pre-conversion experience of someone who knew the law, and especially of himself. The repetition of 'I' and 'me' and the use of the past tense are to be noted. Then, in verses 14-25 he speaks of post conversion experience. The change to the present tense is to be observed.

This last section has three subsections: in verses 14-20, he speaks of struggle, in verses 21-23, of discovery and, in verses 24-25, of crisis. In relation to his struggle, vv. 14-20, we note him saying things like, 'That which I do I allow not', 'What I hate, that do I', 'The good that I would I do not'. In relation to his discovery, vv. 21-23, he says, 'I find', 'I delight', 'I see'. His crisis, vv. 24-25, is marked by the words, 'O wretched man that I am' and 'I thank God'.

Again, we may see that in verses 1-6 Paul states a **fact**: believers are dead to the law by the body of Christ. Then, in verses 7-13 he speaks of **frustration**. Sin got a point of attack and it wrought in him every manner of lust and deceived him. Then, he speaks of a **feud** in verses

14-23, as he indicates that what he does he allows not. Finally, he knows **freedom** through Jesus Christ in the last verses.

Accordingly, in this chapter, Paul looks back, then he looks in and, finally, he looks up.

v. 1   **Know ye not, brethren, (for I speak to them that know the law,) how that the law hath dominion over a man as long as he liveth?**

The apostle establishes that the '**law**' applies only to a living man. Moses' law has only to do with this present life, its terms being summed up in 'the man that doeth them shall live in them', Gal. 3. 12, and, 'the soul that sinneth it shall die', Ezek. 18. 20. These were the unbending terms of the law.

There is no definite article in verse 1 before 'law'. The apostle enunciates the principle of law generally for he will speak of other laws: the law of the husband as well as the law of Moses. Both are the same in that in connection with each there was an 'I will' and both are ended only by death. Law rules or has claims over a man '**as long as he lives**' and only one thing cancels the claims of law, namely death. At death a person is no longer in the sphere where law holds sway for it cannot exercise rule over the dead. It is obviously impossible to serve a summons on a dead man.

v. 2   **For the woman which hath an husband is bound by the law to her husband so long as he liveth; but if the husband be dead, she is loosed from the law of her husband.**

This is now illustrated by the law of marriage, a law which is only cancelled by death. Death alone cancels the marriage contract so that a woman is only discharged from marriage law when her husband dies.

v. 3   **So then if, while her husband liveth, she be married to another man, she shall be called an adulteress: but if her husband be dead, she is free from that law; so that she is no adulteress, though she be married to another man.**

To be married to one man but to belong to another introduces a seriously immoral state of affairs. The deduction is that to put one who belongs to Christ under law is to bring about an adulterous relationship, just as a woman with two husbands. The apostle changes from facts to spiritual teaching.

v. 4   **Wherefore, my brethren, ye also are become dead to the law by the body of Christ; that ye should be married to another, even to him who is raised from the dead, that we should bring forth fruit unto God.**

We have been delivered from the law by the death of Christ. As Christians we have been made dead to law: the passive shows that this is by an external work namely by the '**body of Christ**'. Galatians chapter 4 verse 4 speaks of our Lord as being 'made of a woman, made under the law'. He kept the law in its entirety but in that body, in death, He passed from under its claims. Thus, Paul uses the term the 'body of Christ'. However, to be dead to the law does not involve a life of freedom as we are married to another. We are '**married**' to a risen Christ, so as to '**bring forth fruit**'. The teaching is that we have died to one husband, the law, to be married now to Christ risen from the dead, with fruit in view. Note that the fruit is not to the husband but to God and this is a life dedicated to God. In chapter 6 we are alive to God; in chapter 7 there is fruit to God; in chapter 8 we are enabled for this as we walk by the Spirit.

v. 5   **For when we were in the flesh, the motions of sins, which were by the law, did work in our members to bring forth fruit unto death.**

'**In the flesh**' refers to unconverted and natural men, identified with the old creation, living in a world of sense with no outlook beyond it. The idea is simply that the spirit and the soul are submerged in the flesh and take character from it. This is not the flesh in me, but me in the flesh, being circumscribed by it. Such a man has no knowledge or understanding of the death of Christ. The apostle elaborates on this in chapter 8.

'**Motions**' are passions, sinful passions. Such is the flesh, that the claims of the law only cause it irritation and thus these passions were '**by the law**'. The mind of the flesh, being at enmity with God, is irritated by the law and is in enmity to it. These passions '**did work in our members**' in that they energised the members of our body to go in for fruit unto death, this being the inevitable issue. '**Death**' is physical death. That which was produced in our unregenerate days is temporal and ends in death; it terminates there.

v. 6   **But now we are delivered from the law, that being dead wherein we were held; that we should serve in newness of spirit, and not in the oldness of the letter.**

Man under grace is '**delivered**', or discharged from the law. Note, '**But**'; it is the 'but' of conversion. Here, we are delivered not from the penalty of a broken law but from its claims on our lives, '**having died to that wherein we were held**'. The man in the flesh, over whom law had a claim, has died to its unbending claims. He died in the death of Christ.

'**Spirit**' refers to that which is internal whereas the law is external. '**Newness**' is what is produced upon one's spirit by conversion. The apostle is not here speaking of the Holy Spirit but is rather indicating that the believer does not serve God in the bondage of a law pressed upon an unwilling heart but in novelty of spirit, a joyful state of heart and mind. Law service was reluctant, unintelligent and unwilling, but now regeneration brings newness of spirit. We now serve with joyful heart and mind, gladly and intelligently, not with the mere, blind obedience demanded by the law. Each believer is clear that the works of the law can never save but there are those who strive after holiness and become as legal as possible. However, no flesh will glory in His presence. Therefore, we do not strive for holiness and sanctification by obedience to an obsolete letter but by glad obedience to the revealed mind and will of God. The letter, the moral law, as the rule of life is now obsolete for the Christian; it is antiquated. The ceremonial law is not really in view here. Newness of spirit produces spontaneity in doing the will of God, a glad acknowledgement from the heart. The letter of the law kills in that it brought only rebellion and reluctant obedience. It could never give life but the indwelling Spirit gives life, which is the same principle as in Romans 8.

v. 7   **What shall we say then? Is the law sin? God forbid. Nay, I had not known sin, but by the law: for I had not known lust, except the law had said, Thou shalt not covet.**

Now the apostle speaks of the pre-conversion experience of one who was under the law. 'I' in the verses to verse 13 refers to personal, pre-conversion experience. It is not the experience of every person: rather, it is the experience of a person under the law, with Paul thinking of himself in particular. This section has two questions which sum up its teaching. In verse 7, 'Is the law sin?', and in verse 13 'Is the law death?'.

The question 'Is the law sin?' is raised here because of what the apostle has said in verse 5. Some might have thought that he was teaching that if the passions of sins were by the law then the law is sin. His answer to such a thought is 'God forbid'. In fact the answer to the question raised in this verse is found in verse 12, where the apostle says that the law is holy, just and good.

Paul approaches the matter from the negative standpoint. Speaking of pre-conversion experience, he says that without the law he 'had not known sin', meaning he had not recognised sin. He does not say, 'I had not had sin' but 'I had not known sin'. Sin is there apart from the law because it indwells the heart but sin is aroused by the law and desires what is prohibited by it. Thus, we have seen that in chapter 3 verse 20 he states that 'by the law is the knowledge of sin'. The law had made him aware of that evil principle within him and apart from it he had not known (conscious, intelligent acquaintance) 'lust' or concupiscence. 'Thou shalt not covet', or lust, is the commandment selected by Paul, as lust precedes action. It points to lust as undoubted evidence of indwelling sin.

v. 8   But sin, taking occasion by the commandment, wrought in me all manner of concupiscence. For without the law sin was dead.

This is a difficult verse. 'Concupiscence' is simply lust. The apostle speaks relatively when he says, 'without the law sin was dead'. Sin, though present, was inactive. It took 'occasion by the commandment'; finding by the commandment not to lust an opportunity for action, a ground of attack, and thus it aroused in him a desire for these things. The fact is that when the law is applied to the human heart the principle of indwelling sin is immediately aroused. It is not that sin dies in the forensic sense but rather he speaks comparatively. Unless it is opposed, sin is dead, or torpid as regards its development. The proof of this is in the next verse.

v. 9   For I was alive without the law once: but when the commandment came, sin revived, and I died.

The apostle says that 'without the law I was alive'. In his unconverted days Paul was 'dead', in terms of his being dead in trespasses and sins, but just as sin in verse 8 was not really dead, so Paul in verse

9 was not really alive. He took the ground of being able to live to God but **'when the commandment came'**, that is, when this particular commandment, 'thou shalt not lust', was applied to his condition, **'sin revived'** and he **'died'**. This is not, as some have thought, a reference to conversion but Paul is saying that his assumed ability to live to God was proved to be wrong. Sin was roused from its apparent death and acted again. Then, he died: his assumed ability to live to God in unconverted days was proved wrong. He realised all of this on reflection only after he was converted. All of these terms are comparative. Sin does not actually die: sin is torpid until it comes against the commandment which incites to lust, and the man who thought he was living unto God finds this was not in fact true. Thus, it is death and life comparatively.

v. 10	**And the commandment, which was ordained to life, I found to be unto death.**

The discovery Paul made was that **'the commandment which was ordained to life'** he found **'to be unto death'**. The principle of the law, which was 'this do and thou shalt live' and 'the man that doeth these things shall live in them', Paul, surprisingly, found to be unto death. It exposed his inability to live unto God. Life was offered in the law to those who could keep it but no one was able to do so; accordingly, all who were under the law forfeited the right to live. The law proves man's inability to keep the law of God. That is how the 'law was our schoolmaster unto Christ', Gal. 3. 24; it showed man his absolute need of Christ. The thought in that verse is not 'to bring us unto Christ' but 'until Christ'. His death procured for man what the law never could, namely life.

v. 11	**For sin, taking occasion by the commandment, deceived me, and by it slew me.**

The apostle is continuing to answer the question raised in verse 7. **'Sin'** got a point of attack **'by the commandment'** and **'deceived'** and **'slew'** him. However, the law is not sin; the fault is not with the law at all but with sin and self. 'Sin' deceived 'me'. Sin deceived him in that by means of the commandment it filled his heart with what was forbidden. It suggested to him that if he disobeyed he would be happy. In fact, it slew him, bringing him under the curse of the broken law. Thus, verse 11 states that the law is not at fault; he was deceived by sin.

v. 12   **Wherefore the law is holy, and the commandment holy, and just, and good.**

Paul indicates that the 'law is holy' and therefore not at fault. 'The commandment is holy, and just and good'. God could not have given something that was otherwise. 'Law' is changed to 'commandment'. 'Law' is the law as a whole; 'commandment' is each precept in particular. Note the order: it is holy in its character, just in its demands and good in its purpose.

v. 13   **Was then that which is good made death unto me? God forbid. But sin, that it might appear sin, working death in me by that which is good; that sin by the commandment might become exceeding sinful.**

Here is the second question of this section. '**Is the law death?**' It stems from verse 10 where Paul indicates that he found the commandment to be unto death '**but sin**' was the culprit. It worked out '**death**' in him in that it made him aware of his inability to live unto God and it did so by that which is good. God knew the outcome as far as man was concerned but in terms of man's acceptance before God He must prove conclusively that there is only one ground of acceptance and that is Calvary. The law showed man his utter need of a Saviour, someone outside of himself. Thus, the law really exposed the true nature of sin, sin being made to appear what it really is. The commandment, by virtue of its goodness and righteousness, only provoked sin to rebel and sin then became '**exceeding sinful**'. The law is not death; sin is the culprit. The law simply provoked sin to rebel.

Prior to conversion there is no justification by the law. After conversion there is no sanctification by the law. Man is to learn that as a sinner he can never be saved by the law and that as a saint he can never be practically sanctified by it.

v. 14   **For we know that the law is spiritual: but I am carnal, sold under sin.**

A new section of the chapter begins at this point. In verses 7-13 Paul has been speaking in the past tense about pre-conversion experience but now he uses the present tense in respect of that which is post-conversion.

The 'law is spiritual' in addition to what he says about it in verse 12. It is spiritual in that the demands of the law require an inward state, a spiritual condition for them to be fulfilled. The next chapter states that this is only possible in connection with conversion.

This verse is a problem to some who ask whether it could be true of a child of God that he is 'carnal, sold under sin'. 'Carnal' refers not to the unconverted state of being in the flesh, obeying only the mind of the flesh, nor is its meaning the same as in 1 Corinthians 3 where it describes a Christian who is not spiritually mature. Here 'carnal' is not used in a moral sense at all but simply means that we are formed of flesh. It is, therefore, true of all men. In verse 23 Paul speaks of a law in his members. 'I am carnal' means 'I am still in a body'. We must always keep in mind the context. Paul simply says that as long as he is in the body he will be sold under sin. The mind is not in view.

The term 'sold under sin' refers to being under its influence. Paul does not have any particular act in mind but is stating what will always be true of us as long as we are in the body. Chapter 6 verse 17 is therefore to be distinguished. In chapter 6 we have changed masters but so long as we are in the body in a world where sin reigns we shall be under its influence. Anything short of sinless perfection makes this patent and no one can boast of sinless perfection. We are given all things that pertain to godliness and we are equipped therefore to live for God and in His fear. The reason why we sin is not failure on God's part. In unconverted days we were unaware of the bondage of sin and yielded our members to sin willingly and gladly. Only since conversion is there a real sense of shame. Once a person is saved he has a deeper sense of God's holiness and is possessed of holy desires. He is then more deeply aware of the bondage of sin, something which is explained in verses 15-20.

v. 15   **For that which I do I allow not: for what I would, that do I not; but what I hate, that do I.**

In verses 15-20 Paul speaks of his powerlessness to refrain from doing what he knows to be wrong. This was true of the early days of Paul's Christian testimony. '**That which I do**', or perform, I do not own; I acknowledge it is wrong. In fact, I hate it. What I desire to perform that do I not. All of this is against my renewed mind.

v. 16   **If then I do that which I would not, I consent unto the law that it is good**

If I practise what I desire not, I agree with the law that it is right in forbidding those things.

v. 17   **Now then it is no more I that do it, but sin that dwelleth in me.**

His conclusion is that it is '**no more I that do it, but sin that dwelleth in me**'. This does not mean that he must be excused as it is not him but sin. Rather, prior to conversion he was deceived, but that is no longer so; there is now a feud between sin and myself. I desire to do what is right and I hate what is wrong. When I don't do what my new mind desires, and when I do what my renewed mind hates, it is sin that has won the day. Paul is thinking of a person who is still placing himself under law for a sanctified life. Sin never produces actions unless there is a yielding of the will and so sin of itself can never be blamed if I do wrong. Here, Paul is saying that he was endeavouring to resist sin in his own efforts but that will never work. Note all the uses of 'I'. Practical sanctification is never achieved in this way or in our own strength.

v. 18   **For I know that in me (that is, in my flesh,) dwelleth no good thing: for to will is present with me; but how to perform that which is good I find not.**

Now the apostle speaks of being sold under sin from a different angle. Progress is, in fact, being made. In verses 15-16 he speaks of the operation of the will, 'I allow', 'I would', 'I hate', 'I consent', but now he says 'I know'. I have come to a conclusion which is that in me '**dwelleth no good thing**'. Indwelling sin, he knows, has affected everything, his desires and affection. Good in its perfection does not dwell in him or in his flesh. The truth of this is shown in the middle clause of verse 18; there is a will to do but the power cannot be found to perform it in self effort.

vv. 19-20 **For the good that I would I do not: but the evil which I would not, that I do. Now if I do that I would not, it is no more I that do it, but sin that dwelleth in me.**

The same conclusion he reached in verse 17 is found in verse 20. The apostle is not speaking of a perpetual feud, a general situation, but of a Christian seeking practical sanctification in his own strength. This is the only way you can understand these verses. Sanctification is never found in 'I'.

v. 21   **I find then a law, that, when I would do good, evil is present with me.**

Now the apostle speaks of his discovery. In verse 21, 'I find', in verse 22, 'I delight' and, in verse 23, 'I see'. '**I find a law**' which is that when he wills to practise what is right and good, evil is present. This is not the law of sin in his members, v. 23. In his mind, he wills to obey God's law but the act of obedience is not forthcoming because evil is there. Thus, there is a conflict between his will and his action. There is a law upon him; it is not just in him as a principle but it is bearing upon him in its rightness, its correctness. He is a converted man but this law is bearing upon him in terms of its application. This is divine law, though not Moses' law, that presses upon all those who belong to Christ.

v. 22   **For I delight in the law of God after the inward man:**

In the previous verse he agrees with the law of God that it is right. His mind is in agreement with it. Now, in verse 22, there is progress for he '**delights in the law of God**'. This is as a regenerate man, according to the '**inward man**' by reason of divine quickening. He delights in the law of God as a result of what is now in him. The unregenerate do not delight in the law of God. An unbeliever will be checked by his conscience, something that is negative, but here is something positive, delight in the law of God.

v. 23   **But I see another law in my members, warring against the law of my mind, and bringing me into captivity to the law of sin which is in my members.**

As the result of examination, Paul sees '**another law**'. This law engages in conflict with the law of his renewed mind. The law of that '**mind**' delights in the law of God, but there is another law in conflict with it. Though his mind delights in the law of God, he is brought into captivity, not to sin but to the law of sin. This law is that which always sets sin in the place of authority. This explains verse 14 where the apostle speaks of being carnal, sold under sin.

v. 24   **O wretched man that I am! who shall deliver me
           from the body of this death?**

A crisis is now reached and we hear his cry of distress, **'Who shall
deliver me?'** The body is the base of operations for sin and it is
called **'the body of death'** because though sin will not die its base
of operations, this body, will. It is a mortal body. He does not ask
'how shall I be delivered' but 'who shall deliver me' and as he
could not find the answer in self he must look elsewhere.

v. 25   **I thank God through Jesus Christ our Lord. So
           then with the mind I myself serve the law of God;
           but with the flesh the law of sin.**

Here is the answer to the question of the previous verse: deliverance comes **'through Jesus Christ our Lord'**. The apostle is not
saying 'I thank God through Jesus Christ our Lord' as if in prayer.
Rather, deliverance is through Jesus Christ our Lord and it is both
future and present. It will be known in the future at His coming
and in the present as we look to Christ and not self. Deliverance
can be enjoyed now as the heart is filled with Christ.

Here is Paul's grand conclusion: with the renewed mind he serves
God's law, but with the flesh the law of sin. The law of God is what
is contained in the word of God binding upon us as Christians
rather than the law of Moses. Whilst we are not under the law,
there are principles binding upon us which can never be fulfilled
in our own strength but only as we look to Christ.

THE BELIEVER AND THE HOLY SPIRIT

Chapter 8 verses 1-39

This chapter concludes the doctrinal part of Romans. In verses 1-27 the subject is the believer's life in the Holy Spirit. In chapters 1-7 the Holy Spirit is mentioned only once, in chapter 5 verse 5, but in chapter 8 He is the great theme.

There is no grammatical justification for changing verses 16 and 26 where the King James Version says 'the Spirit itself'. The Revised Version and others say 'the Spirit Himself'. No matter how much we believe, as we do, in the personality of the Holy Spirit these verses must read 'itself'. Paul speaks like this not because he is thinking of the Holy Spirit as a mere influence but because the word for 'spirit' is the Greek word *pneuma* which is a neuter word. Thus, the name given to the Spirit is neuter: it has to do with His mode of operation which is brought before us extensively in this chapter. Notice the references to this: in verses 2, He sets free; verse 4, the believer walks according to the Holy Spirit; verse 13, by the Holy Spirit the believer mortifies the deeds of the body; verse 14, the sons of God are led by the Holy Spirit; verse 16, the Holy Spirit inwardly witnesses that we are the children of God; and verse 26, the Holy Spirit helps our infirmities and makes intercession for us. Of course, the personality of the Holy Spirit is established in this chapter, even though we read the word 'itself'. In verse 27 the apostle speaks of 'the mind of the Spirit' and in verse 26 of the Spirit interceding.

The relationship of chapter 8 to chapters 6 and 7 is just this. In chapter 6 verse 11 we reckon ourselves to be alive unto God in Christ Jesus and we observed in chapter 6 verse 13 that this involves yielding ourselves to God. The teaching of chapter 6 is that I live unto God and I yield myself to God. In chapter 7 verse 4 I bring forth fruit unto God, but just as chapter 6 does not tell me how I can live unto God or how I can yield to Him, for it is purely doctrinal, neither does chapter 7 tell me how I can bring forth fruit unto God. That again is purely doctrinal but chapter 8 furnishes the answer as to how I can do these things; it is by the power of the indwelling Spirit.

The teaching of chapters 6, 7 and 8 may be remembered like this. In chapter 6 Lazarus heard the loud voice of the Son of God saying, 'Lazarus, come forth'. He is alive to God. In chapter 7 Lazarus, though alive, is bound hand and foot with grave clothes and his face is bound with a napkin. John chapter 11 verse 46 answers to Romans chapter 7 verse 19, alive, but in bondage. In chapter 8 we hear the Saviour say, 'Loose him and let him go'. In chapter 8 we are set free; we walk according to the Spirit and we are led by the Spirit.

v. 1   **There is therefore now no condemnation to them which are in Christ Jesus, who walk not after the flesh, but after the Spirit.**

Verses 1-4 relate to what has been said between chapter 5 verse 12 and the end of chapter 7. The believer is no longer under fear of '**condemnation**'. The word '**no**' is emphatic. 'Condemnation' here and in chapter 5 verses 16-18 has reference to our being in Adam. Chapter 5 teaches that Adam's headship does not go back to him in innocence but in sin and that, being in Adam, man is under judgement to condemnation. As being in Adam, the sentence of judgement was passed upon us and this would have issued in eternal condemnation. Now, however, there is no thought or possibility of the condemnation or damnation to which we hasted as being in Adam. Christ Jesus is the head of a new race, not by reason of His incarnation but because of His death, resurrection and exaltation. The fact that we are in Christ Jesus places us beyond reach of damnation and eternal condemnation. Condemnation is penal. However, in Christ there is no condemnation in its penal sense because the sentence of judgement is past and will never be executed on the child of God. For such there is no eternal penalty. In 1 John chapter 4 verse 17, we have no fear of judgement as Christ is at God's right hand, beyond death and judgement. As He is, so are we in this world.

v. 2   **For the law of the Spirit of life in Christ Jesus hath made me free from the law of sin and death.**

This verse sums up chapter 6. There we were under the law of sin and death in unconverted days. Sin was a relentless master whose wages were death but we died with Christ to sin and are now justified from it. In chapter 6 we are not freed from sin's penalty but freed from it as a master. So now he speaks of having been '**made free from the law of sin and death**'. The aorist is used: this relates

to a thing that happened once and for all and is complete in itself
and thus it takes us back to conversion. We were then made free
but we are now under a new law, the law of the Spirit of life in
Christ Jesus. 'In Christ Jesus' is the position into which grace has
put every believer and that position is eternally secure. However,
it is not only a position, for the apostle speaks of 'life' in Christ
Jesus. There is a life associated with that new position. The 'Spirit'
is the power of that life, the power in which that life is enjoyed.
'Law' is any given principle which acts in a uniform fashion, such
as gravity. The Spirit always acts in a uniform way and the apostle
goes on to explain what he means by that when he speaks, in verse
4, of walking according to the Spirit and, in verse 5, of minding the
things of the Spirit. Thus, we have been introduced to a new freedom, the law of the Spirit of life in Christ Jesus. The law of the
Spirit is not a law that binds but a law that brings power. By it we
have power to obey what God requires in His word. This life that
we have in Christ Jesus we possess now but we shall enjoy it
eternally.

Notice that in verse 1 it is 'them' but it is 'me' in verse 2. 'Them' has
to do with what is positional but 'me' is experiential. In verse 1,
I am in Christ Jesus with everyone: in verse 2, it is very personal.

v. 3   **For what the law could not do, in that it was weak
           through the flesh, God sending his own Son in
           the likeness of sinful flesh, and for sin,
           condemned sin in the flesh:**

These verses sum up chapter 7. In that chapter Paul wrote to
those who 'know the law', particularly the Jews. In chapter 8, he
reminds them of what they knew: they knew '**what the law could
not do**' and they knew what grace had done. The apostle makes it
clear in these verses that failure under the law was nothing to do
with the law itself. There was complete failure under the law
because of the material the law had to work upon. The law said
'thou shalt not' and man could not resist: it said 'thou shalt' and
man could not perform. The law could not procure the fulfilment
of its demands '**in that it was weak through flesh**'; it was weak
through human frailty but it was not weak in itself. God did not
have to deal with the law but with the man in the flesh who could
not keep the law. We observed, in chapter 7, that the law is holy
and just and good.

Hebrews speaks of the weakness and unprofitableness of the law and Galatians of the weak and beggarly elements, so that the New Testament three times speaks of the weakness of the law. I repeat, this was not an inherent weakness but weakness through the flesh. However, the 'power of God' is connected to the gospel in three chapters, namely Romans 1, 1 Corinthians 1 and Ephesians 1.

God dealt with man in the flesh by **'sending His own Son in the likeness of sinful flesh, and for sin'**. In this connection compare verse 32, where the apostle again speaks of 'His own Son', though 'His own' is a slightly different phrase in each verse. Here, it is the dearness of His Son that Paul has in mind. He came 'in likeness of flesh of sin', a reference to the Son of God's incarnation. He did not come in the likeness of flesh, for it was real flesh, though not sinful flesh. God sent His Son not in flesh of sin but in the likeness of flesh of sin. The Spirit of God is always careful to assert that the manhood of Christ was perfect; it was unique. There was no sin in His flesh for 'in Him is no sin', 1 John 3. 5. God carefully guards the impeccability of His Son. Sin has been condemned by one in the flesh who has been here, who Himself knew no sin. God sent Him 'for sin', 'for' having a sacrificial sense, as in Hebrews chapter 10 verse 8. The idea is 'as a sacrifice for sin'. Thus, at Calvary God judged sin in One in whom there is no sin. Paul introduces this because it is necessary for what he is going to speak of in the next verse, namely the receiving of the Holy Spirit.

'**Condemned'** has in view not just that the sentence was passed but that it was also executed in a man in whom there is no sin. It is important to understand that for God to condemn sin in the flesh two things were necessary. There was a need not just for a sacrifice for sin but for one made by a man in whom there was no sin. There was a man here who kept the law and made it honourable. Both our Lord's incarnation and death are in view here. When the apostle speaks of 'God sending His own Son in the likeness of sinful flesh', he speaks of His incarnation: when he says, 'and for sin' the necessity of Calvary is presented.

v. 4   **That the righteousness of the law might be fulfilled in us, who walk not after the flesh, but after the Spirit.**

God had to condemn sin in the flesh by the sacrifice of Calvary because there had not been a man here in the flesh in whom there was no sin. This having been accomplished He has now sent down the Holy Spirit into our hearts **'that the righteousness of the law might be fulfilled in us'**. Walking **'after the Spirit'** and not **'after the flesh'** has in view not walking by the rule or principle of the flesh but as the Spirit guides or controls. The righteousness of the law is fulfilled in us. This does not mean the requirements of the law in their absolute sense for if that happened, the law being totally fulfilled by us, there would be sinless perfection involved. Paul does not speak of the righteous requirements being fulfilled 'by' us, as having been set before us in terms of what God requires, but of them being fulfilled 'in' us, quite unconsciously as we walk guided and controlled by the Holy Spirit. A Christian cannot be under law and grace at the same time. The relationship of the law to the Christian is that God does not set it before us as the principle by which we should live. He has given us His Spirit, and as we walk according to the Spirit the righteous requirements of the law are fulfilled in us. Thus, it is important to note that it is 'in us' not 'by us'.

Once we walked in the flesh and knew nothing else, but now we walk after the Spirit. The Spirit is the sphere in which we walk: 'walking after the Spirit', or according to the Spirit, is walking after the Spirit's directions and leading.

God has done through His Son what the law could never do. He dealt with everything in us that hindered the reception of the Spirit and the power to live for God. Sin in the flesh always acts contrary to the claims of the law and in an adverse way. Note the force of **'that'**. Before God could send into our hearts His Spirit, the power by which the requirements of the law are fulfilled in us, it was necessary that sin was dealt with by one in whom there is no sin and who made a sacrifice for sin. Unbelievers can do nothing other than walk after the flesh but the believer walks after the Spirit.

All this is illustrated from John 5 in the incident of the man at the pool of Bethesda who had had an infirmity for thirty-eight years. The angel causing the trembling of the water speaks of the law. (The law given by the disposition of angels, Acts 7; it was ordained by angels in the hands of a mediator, Galatians 3; it was the word spoken by angels, Hebrews 2). Thirty-eight years was the time that Israel was in the wilderness under the law. However, the angel troubling the waters had no benefit to the man who had no power to get into the pool. The law was weak through the flesh but when God's Son came and said, 'Take up thy bed and walk', we see the idea of the requirements of the law being fulfilled in us.

There are three sections in the verses 5-23, each section ending with the future glory of the children of God. In verse 11 our bodies are quickened at the Lord's coming; in verse 17 we are glorified together; and, in verse 23, we receive sonship, complete conformity to the image of Christ, at His coming again.

The subject matter of verses 5-11 is highlighted in verse 10. As long as we are here, we are to keep this body in the place of death because of sin so as to produce righteousness in the power of the Spirit. The day will come when there will be no need to keep the body in the place of death because of sin; in verse 11 these mortal bodies will be quickened at the Lord's coming and will no longer be the vehicles of sin, bodies that sin delights to use. The apostle tells us that the pledge of this future quickening is the indwelling Spirit.

If the subject matter of verses 5-11 is doctrinal then verses 12-17 contain the practical outworking of it. In verse 13 the apostle says that if we mortify the deeds of the body, put them to death at their inception, we shall live. This refers not to the future but to living now. As we mortify the deeds of the body we live now in peace and true joy and to God. Verses 14-16 sum up what is meant by 'ye shall live'; it is being led by the Spirit, v. 14, and crying 'Abba Father', v. 16. In this verse, the apostle speaks of the inward witness of the Holy Spirit. This is life! Men of the world know nothing of this. Though we suffer, the witness of the Spirit is that we are the children of God. We enjoy life that is life indeed. This does not give us immunity from suffering yet despite it we have the assurance of being heirs of God and joint heirs with Christ and of one day being glorified together with Him. This makes the enduring of present suffering all the more easy.

'Present sufferings and future glory' is the theme of verses 18-23. In verse 18 the apostle speaks of the 'glory which shall be revealed in us'. Notice, 'groaning' and 'waiting' are referred to twice. Creation groans and waits. It has been said that the sighing of the wind, the groaning of the sea, the bleating of the sheep and the lowing of cattle remind us that the whole song of creation is in a minor key. It is groaning and travailing in the birth pangs of a day that is yet to be, a day spoken of in verse 19 as the day of the manifestation of the sons of God at our Lord's appearing in glory. Believers also groan and wait in this section, v. 23. The redemption of the body is connected with future glory when He comes again. We groan because our bodies still form part of an unredeemed creation; our souls are redeemed now but not our bodies. We wait for this, but in the meantime we groan because our bodies are bodies of humiliation identified with a groaning creation. We are waiting for the sonship, the redemption of the body, when it will no longer be a body of humiliation but a body of glory. Thus, we groan and we wait.

v. 5   **For they that are after the flesh do mind the things of the flesh; but they that are after the Spirit the things of the Spirit.**

In this section, the apostle is not speaking of carnal and spiritual Christians, as he does in 1 Corinthians 3, but concerning the matter of being in the Spirit or in the flesh. All believers are in the Spirit; all unbelievers are in the flesh. Note verse 9: 'ye are not in the flesh but in the Spirit'. In the Spirit is not as in Revelation chapter 1 verse 10. Being in the Spirit, v. 9, is true of every believer. We accept, and rightly so, that the Spirit of God dwells in every believer and because that is true 'you are not in the flesh'. It is most important to notice that we are in the Spirit because the Spirit is in us. Paul will develop this truth. The 'but' of verse 9 is the 'but' of conversion. If 'in the Spirit' is true of every believer, 'in the flesh' is true of every unbeliever. As for the believer, the child of God, the flesh is in him but he is not in the flesh. Every Christian has the indwelling Spirit of God and is 'in the Spirit', meaning that he is in that sphere now where he is under the rule and influence of the Holy Spirit. As to the unbeliever he is in the flesh. The apostle does not mean that the unbeliever is in the flesh corporeally, in a body, for that is true of all men. In Galatians he speaks of 'the life which I now live in the flesh', or 'the life I live in a body'. Neither does he mean simply that he is in Adam, as being his child, or in the flesh as being possessed of a corrupt life which has a will not according to God's will. Rather, he is characterised by the flesh and controlled by it and so the Bible speaks of the 'will of the flesh' and the 'mind of the flesh'. However, the believer is no longer in the flesh as we saw in chapter 7 verse 5, when Paul speaks of the time 'when we were in the flesh'. Now the believer is in the Spirit. Thus, in verses 5-11 the apostle sets out to show the sharp contrast between the regenerate and the unregenerate. Unless we see this we shall never understand the section.

Thus, in verse 5, there is a contrast as to persons and as to their aim. 'They that are after', or according to, the flesh, have the flesh as their rule of life. They 'mind', a strong word, the things of the flesh, not simply in terms of being influenced or tempted by the flesh but having a preference for it; they are fully absorbed by, and are engrossed in all that this corrupt life of the flesh desires. The regenerate, however, are not simply influenced by the Spirit but pursue the things of the Spirit: this is the bent of their lives.

v. 6   For to be carnally minded is death; but to be
           spiritually minded is life and peace.

Again, it is important to see that the apostle is not here speaking of carnal Christians. Such an interpretation is impossible. The expression 'to be carnally minded is death' has the idea that 'the mind of the flesh is death'. Paul is still speaking of the unregenerate who are possessed only of the mind of the flesh, which is legal death in terms of their eternal doom. The unregenerate will pass from spiritual death to eternal death. In contrast to death 'the mind of the Spirit', where every believer is in view, not just the spiritually minded, is life and peace. Life is communion with God; peace and tranquility is that which is enjoyed in the heart as a present experience. There is, then, a contrast in the effect of the mind of the flesh and the mind of the Spirit.

vv. 7-8   Because the carnal mind is enmity against God:
           for it is not subject to the law of God, neither
           indeed can be. So then they that are in the flesh
           cannot please God.

There are two statements made here: positively, the apostle states that the mind of the flesh is enmity against God; and, negatively, that those who are in the flesh cannot please God. There is positive hostility to God, reminding us of chapter 5 verse 10: believers were once enemies in the flesh. As such they were incapable of pleasing God. Two intervening statements in verse 7 are explanatory. The mind of the flesh is not subject to the law of God in its demands, whether they be Godward or manward and it is incorrigible. Unregenerate man might be religious and philanthropic, apparently well disposed toward God and kindly toward men, but here the apostle is not speaking of works but of the mind, of motive and disposition. Only what is done by the regenerate, therefore, is acceptable to God. All this is very sorry language.

v. 9   **But ye are not in the flesh, but in the Spirit, if so be that the Spirit of God dwell in you. Now if any man have not the Spirit of Christ, he is none of his.**

What is stated here is true only of a Christian. The Christian is '**not in the flesh but in the Spirit**'. This is different from Revelation chapter 1 verse 10 where John was in the Spirit on the Lord's Day. Romans 8 is positional truth and what is stated is true of every believer. The Christian is in the Spirit because the Spirit is in the Christian. '**But**' is the 'but' of conversion. '**In the Spirit**' is true of every believer: '**in the flesh**' is true of every unbeliever. Though the flesh is in the Christian, the Christian is no longer in the flesh. Thus, the regenerate man is in view.

The '**Spirit of God**' and the '**Spirit of Christ**' is within the believer. Both expressions speak of the same person. He is the Spirit of God, God being the giver; He is the Spirit of Christ, Christ being the dispenser. God gives and Christ dispenses the Holy Spirit. In John chapter 4 verse 10 our Saviour said, 'If thou knewest the gift of God, (the Holy Spirit) and who it is that saith to thee, Give me to drink; thou wouldest have asked of him, (the Son of God) and he would have given thee living water'. Again, in verse 14, He says, 'the water that I shall give him shall be in him a well of water springing up into everlasting life'. Thus, the Spirit is the gift and Christ is the dispenser, something also true of eternal life.

Also, the Spirit of Christ is the one who reveals Christ to the believer and through the believer. Christ is in you by the Spirit of God, '**if any man have not the Spirit of Christ, he is none of his**'. We might have expected Paul to say that if any man has not the 'Spirit of God' he is none of His, but he speaks of the 'Spirit of Christ'. This is because the apostle is speaking of the matter of being able to say who belongs to Christ and who does not. We cannot see the Spirit of God in each other but we can see the Spirit of Christ as He replicates Christ in me. This is the evidence that I am His.

v. 10   **And if Christ be in you, the body is dead because of sin; but the Spirit is life because of righteousness.**

'**If**', better 'since' as there is no doubt expressed, '**Christ be in you**', by His Spirit, the '**body is dead on account of sin**'; that is, the body, as a vehicle of sin, is kept in the place of death. However, the '**Spirit is life because of righteousness**'. The apostle is not thinking here of the quickened spirit of the believer but of the Spirit of God. The Spirit is life because of righteousness, not in terms of the believer having been reckoned righteous but rather He produces what is consistent with God's character and of Christ in the believer. Thus, Paul speaks of practical righteousness.

v. 11   **But if the Spirit of him that raised up Jesus from the dead dwell in you, he that raised up Christ from the dead shall also quicken your mortal bodies by his Spirit that dwelleth in you.**

In thinking of the quickening of the mortal body we need to be clear that it is not resurrection in view, for the mortal body is a living body, not a dead one. See chapter 6 verse 12 for another reference to the mortal body to prove this. He says that though this mortal body, as the vehicle of sin, has to be kept now in the place of death it will not always be so. It will be quickened when the Lord Jesus Christ comes again. The same indwelling Spirit who is life now, for we have to reckon the body is dead, is the pledge of the future quickening at the coming again of the Lord Jesus Christ. Mortality shall be swallowed up of life and every impediment to enjoying eternal life will be removed, for then the spirit and body will be in total agreement.

We look at verse 11 like this: 'But if the Spirit of Him (God) that raised up Jesus from the dead dwell in you, He (God) shall also quicken (not raise) your mortal bodies by His Spirit that dwelleth in you'. '**By** (*dia*) **His Spirit**' is 'on account of' or 'because of' His Spirit and thus the indwelling Spirit is the present pledge that our mortal bodies will be quickened and that there will be removed every impediment to the enjoyment of eternal life. Since the Spirit is the pledge of this the apostle is not speaking of resurrection; He does not dwell in a corpse but in these mortal bodies.

Notice the word '**also**'. The apostle uses this word to show that whilst our spirits are quickened at the present time, our bodies will also be quickened at the rapture. Notice also that the verse speaks of '**Jesus**' raised and of '**Christ**' raised. The raising of Jesus is historic; the raising of Christ has in view His being raised as our representative. Notice, then, the beautiful accuracy of the word of God in these distinctions. Our spirits are quickened now, but the day is coming when our bodies will be eternally suited to our quickened spirits. Then, we will no longer have to keep our bodies in the place of death; no longer will we have to mortify the members of our body.

We may ask the question as to why the apostle uses 'quickened' and not 'changed'. Of course, our spirit is not changed. Our spirit is quickened and our body is quickened in conformity to our quickened spirit. Paul is not speaking here in terms of the change of our body of humiliation to a body of glory, nor with our conformity to Christ, which he deals with in the next section, but with the quickening of our mortal body which will happen at the rapture.

If, in verses 5-11, the apostle has spoken doctrinally of the difference between the believer and unbeliever, he speaks in verses 12-17 of the practical outworking of it in the life of the believer. Notice, the emphasis on the believer. In verse 12 he speaks of 'brethren'; in verse 14 of 'sons of God'; and in verse 15 of 'children of God'. What a lovely three-fold designation of every child of God!

v. 12   **Therefore, brethren, we are debtors, not to the flesh, to live after the flesh.**

As '**brethren**' we owe nothing to the '**flesh**'. The 'old man' relates to us in our Adam standing, something which was terminated by God judicially at the cross. The flesh is that corrupt life connected to our Adam standing. We are no longer in the flesh, controlled by it and characterised by its will and mind though the flesh is still in us. The flesh is the corrupt life that every one has by natural generation. In relation to God it is dead, hostile, insubject and incorrigible. We owe nothing to it to live after it. Believers are not 'in' the flesh positionally nor should they be 'after' it, which refers to their manner of life.

v. 13   **For if ye live after the flesh, ye shall die: but if ye through the Spirit do mortify the deeds of the body, ye shall live.**

In the expression '**if ye live after the flesh, ye shall die**' the apostle thinks back to the unregenerate. All who live after the flesh are 'about to die'; such are on the way to physical and eternal death. Paul uses 'ye' even though the unbeliever is in view because he is putting the truth of verse 9 to the test. The setting is that you are His or you are not His. If you live after the flesh death is the ultimate end but if you live after the Spirit you are Christ's.

If, in verse 12, we owe nothing to the flesh, we now owe it to God to put to death the deeds of the body. The verb '**do mortify**' is in the present continuous tense; we will have to do this as long as we live. Every tendency of the body to sin is to be put to death at its inception and every child of God has the power to do this **'through the Spirit'**. Thus, every believer is able to deal with sin in the members of the body at its inception. If this happens **'ye shall live'**; this is not the assurance of future life or eternal life but refers to living now in peace, in communion with heaven, life which is life indeed. To enjoy life now, in terms of peace and communion, we have to use the power God has made available to mortify the deeds of the body. If as a Christian I do not mortify the deeds of the body I will be in a torpid state of spiritual slumber.

The question might be asked as to how we mortify the deeds of the body. Sin is within and around us; the flesh is within and therefore temptation to sin is present. When it arises I must seek the help of the Holy Spirit to kill off desire at its inception. We can only do this if we are minding the things of the Spirit. In Colossians 3, we are exhorted to mortify the members of our body. Colossians tells us, as a matter of doctrine, that we have died and that we are to keep our members in the state of death but we need Romans 8 to tell us by what means we are to do it. Colossians 3 contrasts things above and our members on the earth. As we are taken up with things above, in the power of the Spirit, so we shall keep our members in the place of death.

v. 14   **For as many as are led by the Spirit of God, they are the sons of God.**

The bliss of such a life is now explained. In verse 14 we are 'led by the Spirit' and in verse 15 we are possessed of a spirit of sonship, producing within us the very feelings of a son in which our hearts rise to God and cry 'Abba, Father'.

'As many as are led' does not mean that some Christians are sons of God and some are not. This is the ideal and the ideal includes all believers. Galatians chapter 3 verse 26 indicates that we are all the sons of God through faith. The leading of the Spirit does not make one a child of God and accordingly the article is omitted. It thus reads, **'these are sons of God'**. The leading of the Spirit of God in our lives makes us characteristically what we are by faith. We are by faith sons of God but we become that characteristically in our lives as we deal with everything that hinders the Spirit of God from being in complete control. The Holy Spirit never leads contrary to the Word. In John 17 our Saviour spoke of the word of truth but in John 16 He spoke of the Spirit of truth. One cannot be contrary to the other. Disobedience to the word makes nonsense of any claim to be led by the Holy Spirit.

v. 15 **For ye have not received the spirit of bondage again to fear; but ye have received the Spirit of adoption, whereby we cry, Abba, Father.**

Yielding to the leading of the Holy Spirit is not a grinding surrender, done reluctantly because of a slavish fear, but the response of filial love. Thus, we have not received what characterised those who were under the law, namely a '**spirit of bondage**'. For these there was a continual fear of condemnation through failure, a spirit of bondage, subjection to legal direction and prohibition, but Christianity is not a repetition of this. Note the word, '**again**': you have not received again what you knew under the law. Rather, you have received a '**spirit of sonship**'. This is the operation of the Holy Spirit on our spirits. In Galatians 4 we have the Spirit of His Son but here the apostle refers to our own spirits. In Romans 8, we cry 'Abba, Father' because we have a spirit of sonship; in Galatians 4, the Spirit cries 'Abba, Father'.

The term 'children of God' implies a generative change. 'Sons of God' implies a legal change. We are sons not just by birth but legally and adoptively. A man may adopt into the family and lavish love upon that child but he can never alter that child's descent or give it his own nature. What man cannot do, however, God does. Sonship is the highest form of liberty. The believer has received a spirit of sonship and is able to cry in intercession or worship, '**Abba, Father**'. A slave could never say, 'Abba, Father'. A spirit of bondage causes fear; a spirit of sonship produces a filial heart cry. We are sons now by faith in Christ and the leading of the Spirit makes us to be this characteristically. Sonship in all its fullness is not ours yet; this consists in total conformity to the image of Christ. Thus, we are sons of God by faith now but we express that dignity only as we are led by the Spirit.

'Abba' is Aramaic, 'Father' is Greek and here is something which includes both Jew and Gentile. We must note also that untranslated Aramaic in Scripture speaks of deep feeling and deep pathos. Examples of this are: 'Anathema, Maranatha', 'Eli, Eli, lama sabachthani'. There is a line of teaching, resulting in irreverence in prayer and worship, in which it is said that 'Abba' means 'Daddy' and that God may be addressed as such. Our hearts may well recoil at this. 'Abba' is not the lisping of an infant but the heart cry of a son. Our Lord did not say 'Daddy', in Mark 14 in the Garden, He said 'Abba'. Let us be reverent in our prayers and where we have a choice of language let us always use the more reverent. This is not just a matter of grammar but of reverence. The Saviour was heard in that He feared.

v. 16   **The Spirit itself beareth witness with our spirit, that we are the children of God:**

In this verse the apostle speaks not of sons but of '**children**'. As sons we are led by the Spirit but as children the Spirit bears joint '**witness with** (not 'to') **our spirit**' that we are the children of God now, and joint heirs with Christ in a future inheritance. His witness is along with our own spirits and is confirmatory, giving to us feelings of that real relationship we have with God. This is an inward witness to a great, generative change which makes pointless, futile, wasteful and worthless anything the world might give.

The apostle follows this reference to joint witness with references in verse 17 to joint heirship, joint suffering and joint glorification.

v. 17   **And if children, then heirs; heirs of God, and joint-heirs with Christ; if so be that we suffer with him, that we may be also glorified together.**

In Galatians we are heirs 'through' Christ but here '**with**' Christ. 'Through' refers to His agency. The inheritance is His righteously but it is ours by grace. If we are children, and he has already established the truth of this, then just as surely we are heirs.

'**If so be we suffer with**' does not have the thought that some of the children of God will not suffer. Divine life will ensure this. This is not the suffering of a soldier but of a child and by reason of birth ties. It is not suffering 'for', but 'with'. If I am a child I'll suffer with Him. Those things that grieve Him grieve me too. '**Glorified**' cannot be limited to any particular event; it is a simple contrast to what is here now on earth and describes a state where we shall no longer be suffering in a hostile world.

Verses **18-27** deal with the subject of groaning and waiting. Creation waits, v. 19, and groans, v. 22. The children of God groan and wait, v. 23. As the children of God we are waiting for the moment when we shall receive the sonship when our Lord Jesus Christ comes again. As for creation, it awaits the moment when we shall be revealed with our Saviour at His appearing as the sons of God.

In verses **18-23** the theme is present suffering and future glory. Suffering extends beyond the believer to the whole creation, v. 22. In this section the apostle has more than a quickened body, v. 11, and glorification, v. 17, in view. There is now involved the revelation of that glory, v. 18, and the revelation of the sons of God at His appearing, v. 19. Further, verse 21 speaks of the glorious liberty of the children of God. All the creation is suffering now and waits with outstretched neck for the manifestation of the sons of God.

v. 18   **For I reckon that the sufferings of this present time are not worthy to be compared with the glory which shall be revealed in us.**

The sufferings of '**this present time**' give rise to the children of God groaning, v. 23. Though our spirits have been redeemed and are thus fit for heaven, our bodies are not yet redeemed, and still belong to a groaning creation. The child of God is still subject to those things that affect the rest of the human race, things that are the result of the fall. We are not immune from illness or death. We groan!

The '**glory which shall be revealed in us**' is very embracive and is not to be tied to any one event. We are now sons of God by faith but we wait for sonship in all its fullness; this includes physical conformity to Christ, v. 29. In verse 19, however, it is our being manifested to the world as the sons of God that is in view. For this creation waits and will be delivered from its bondage at that time.

v. 19   **For the earnest expectation of the creature waiteth for the manifestation of the sons of God.**

In the following three verses there are three statements made about creation which should be noted. In verse 20 it is said that '**the creature was made subject to vanity**'. Verse 21 tells us that creation finds itself in '**the bondage of corruption**' and verse 22 indicates that the '**whole creation groaneth and travaileth in pain together until now**'.

As the next verses indicate, there will be a deliverance from this condition and it will occur at '**the manifestation of the sons of God**', something for which creation waits with '**earnest expectation**'. The idea in this word is that of a person with an outstretched neck scanning the sky with hope. Today, we are the sons of God by faith and having received a spirit of sonship we cry 'Abba, Father'. At our Lord's coming we shall receive sonship in all its fullness and know the redemption of our bodies. At His appearing, however, we shall be manifested with Him as sons of God to the wondering eyes of creation and the men and women in the world.

Creation must wait for this event because it was when man fell that creation was delivered into its bondage. Not until man is shown to creation again, redeemed not only in soul but in body, will creation be delivered. The ways of God are so wonderful!

v. 20   **For the creature was made subject to vanity, not willingly, but by reason of him who hath subjected the same in hope,**

Creation's whole existence today is devoid of meaning, purpose and incentive as it has been made '**subject to vanity**'. Two statements are made as to this. First, creation's will played no part in its present condition; '**not willingly**' means that it was not of its own will. Further, it was '**by reason of him**' (God). God brought it about and subjected it to its present condition.

We might ask why He did this. It was necessary because man was placed by God in the beginning as the head of His creation. Only man bears the image of God; man in the Garden was the head of God's creation and over it he exercised dominion. It would have been intolerable to have a fallen man among an unfallen creation. To have man in sin and bondage and creation in liberty would have presented an impossible situation and thus it was necessary for God to bring it into bondage.

The present bondage of creation is not, however, permanent. God subjected it '**in hope**'. Notice, also, that in verse 22 the 'whole creation groaneth and travaileth in pain together until now'. These conditions are but the birth pangs of its ultimate deliverance.

v. 21   **Because the creature itself also shall be delivered from the bondage of corruption into the glorious liberty of the children of God.**

Creation finds itself now in the '**bondage of corruption**', the inevitable result of a purposeless existence, but it will be delivered from '**bondage**' into '**liberty**' and from '**corruption**' into the '**glory**' of the children of God. As we wait for the rapture so creation waits on our appearing as sons of God.

v. 22   **For we know that the whole creation groaneth and travaileth in pain together until now.**

It cannot be gainsaid that the '**whole creation groaneth and travaileth in pain together until now**'. It has been said that the whole of creation is in a minor key.

v. 23   **And not only they, but ourselves also, which have the firstfruits of the Spirit, even we ourselves groan within ourselves, waiting for the adoption, to wit, the redemption of our body.**

As the children of God we have the '**firstfruits of the Spirit**': He now indwells us. As believers we have anticipated the day when God shall pour out of His Spirit upon all flesh, Joel 2. 28. Again, we are '**waiting for the adoption**' or 'the sonship'. We are now sons of God, v. 14, and we have received a spirit of sonship, v. 15, but we wait for sonship in its fullest sense. This involves physical conformity to the image of Christ. The apostle speaks of this again in verse 29 where he states that we shall be 'conformed to the image of his Son'. At the present time our bodies have been purchased by His blood, for they belong to Christ, but they are not yet redeemed. At the rapture these bodies will be redeemed by power. We wait for the sonship, the '**redemption of the body**'.

vv. 24-25 **For we are saved by hope: but hope that is seen is not hope: for what a man seeth, why doth he yet hope for? But if we hope for that we see not, then do we with patience wait for it.**

Our salvation offers us nothing down here, in the sense that it does not give us any promise of exemption from the lot of fallen man in a cursed world. We wait for the realisation of our hope. The apostle tells us that we now exercise patience. God offers nothing down here; the best is yet to be.

vv. 26-27 **Likewise the Spirit also helpeth our infirmities: for we know not what we should pray for as we ought: but the Spirit itself maketh intercession for us with groanings which cannot be uttered.**

> And he that searcheth the hearts knoweth what
> is the mind of the Spirit, because he maketh
> intercession for the saints according to the will
> of God.

In these two verses there are two intercessors who intercede on our behalf. In verse 26 there is the Holy Spirit and in verse 27 there is the Lord. The Spirit is in our hearts and the Lord is on the throne. In John chapter 14 verse 16, our Saviour said, 'I will pray the Father, and he shall give you another Comforter'. The Comforter was not to be instead of the Lord Jesus Christ but in addition to Him. Thus, we have two advocates and the idea in 'another' is another of the same sort, a reference to the deity of the Holy Spirit.

J. N. DARBY translates, 'the Spirit joins also its help to our weakness'. Creation groans together but the Spirit of God 'joins its help to our weakness' and so, today, we have an unspeakable advantage over it. Additionally, we have the advantage that our Lord who '**searcheth the hearts knoweth what is the mind of the Spirit**'. The Holy Spirit takes our groanings and presents them intelligently to the Lord who sits on the throne.

Chapter 8 verses 28-39
In verses 28-30 we love God; in verses 31-34 God loved us; in verses 35-39 there is nothing that can separate us from the love of God.

v. 28   **And we know that all things work together for
             good to them that love God, to them who are the
             called according to his purpose.**

'**We know**' stands in contrast to verse 26, 'we know not'. It is an emphatic statement of truth known by revelation rather than experience.

We might ask what the '**all things**' are to which the apostle refers. Are they every-day events, good and bad, ill or pleasing? Do they include sickness and problems? Do good and bad things work together for good? What 'good' does the apostle speak of, present good or eternal good? Are there distinctions between the people of God in that some love Him and some do not? These are important matters.

In Scripture the word 'all', as in this phrase, is never without qualification. See, for example, Ephesians chapter 1 verse 10, Colossians chapter 1 verse 20 and 1 Corinthians chapter 3 verse 21, among many examples. The expression is always to be understood in context. It does not refer here to those things mentioned in verses 38-39, circumstances of life be they good or bad, but rather as is amplified in verse 29, where the word 'for' means 'because'. An explanation is given. The apostle is stating that these five things all work together for our good. We must beware lest we make shipwreck of the faith of another by quoting this verse glibly.

How do these 'all things' work together? Foreknowledge and predestination occurred in the past, glorification is future and calling and justification are in the present. These are all working together with no disruption, delay or discrepancy and so all are spoken of in the past tense. There is a perfect blending of divine purpose and in God's sight all believers are now all of these things. Thus, we may enjoy this truth experimentally by seeing that there can be no 'fall away' doctrine in Scripture. None will fail. Further, we may learn that there is a dignity in preaching in which we actually play a part in the divine programme. Thus, 'for good' refers not so much to our temporal but to our eternal good. Nothing can thwart His purpose for good for you and me.

In the expression 'them that love God' there is no differentiation between Christians being made. In John's writings those who are born of God love God. In the family we love the Father who begat and will love those who are begotten of Him. What is stated in chapter 5 verse 9, 'we were enemies', is not true of us now. 1 Corinthians chapter 2 verse 9 speaks of that which is 'prepared for them that love Him'. Reference may also be made to 1 Corinthians chapter 8 verse 3, 'If any man love God'. Again, Ephesians chapter 6 verse 24 speaks of 'them that love our Lord Jesus Christ'.

Those who love God are the same as 'them that are called'. This confirms that the expression refers to all Christians. Our love for God might not always be white hot but we do love Him. The effectual call produces love to God. This epistle opens with an effective call, 1. 7, and now concludes its doctrinal section by reference to the same call. This is not the universal call of the gospel but God's effectual call according to His purpose. Many hear the general call of the gospel but do not respond but this is not what is in view here. Here, it is a special call 'according to his purpose'.

v. 29   **For whom he did foreknow, he also did**
         predestinate to be conformed to the image of
         his Son, that he might be the firstborn among
         many brethren.

With the mention of 'foreknowledge' we see that divine purpose is not an afterthought with God. His foreknowledge is involved in His purpose. Note the connection with verse 28, 'we know'; in verse 29 God foreknows. Foreknowledge and predestination are linked to a dateless and timeless past. These are not the same. Foreknowledge relates to persons: predestination refers to the position of blessing marked out for persons. Foreknowledge is not mere prescience, for there is nothing and no one whom God does not know. It is not foreknowledge of facts or of each person in the human race but of persons who are the objects for God's blessings. The verse is stating that God foreknew me, not that He foreknew facts about me.

'**Predestination**' means to mark out beforehand and the word is used only of God, cf. Acts 4. 28; 1 Cor. 2. 7; Eph. 1. 5, 11. The whole matter from the divine side, from eternity to eternity, is here shown. As an individual I am foreknown to God and marked out to be like His Son. Predestination is neither to faith nor unbelief, neither to heaven nor to hell but to be like His Son. Anything less than this would not satisfy God's heart.

The purpose of this call is to be '**conformed to the image of his Son**'. God's purpose always centres in His Son. This will be adoption in all its fullness and is a theme running through the New Testament, cf. Phil. 3. 20; 1 Cor. 15. 51; 1 John 3. 2; Heb. 2. 10. We wait for the sonship. This surpasses the Edenic likeness and image in which man was made and is something possible only by reason of Calvary. These are blessings to man which it would not be possible to have otherwise.

This conformity is a complete inward and outward transformation, a purpose grand in design and great in extent. We shall never, of course, be God as was promised by the serpent to Eve. Man has always desired to be God and this will manifest itself fully in a coming day, 2 Thess. 2. 4. Adam was made in God's image, Gen. 1. 27, but this was tarnished by sin and so in Genesis chapter 5 verse 3 Adam begat a son 'after his image'. We have Adam's fallen nature. However, the Lord Jesus Christ is the image of the invisible God. His image is secured in Him. All who trust Him are His brethren and all such will be conformed to His image.

We shall be conformed to the image of His Son that He might be the **'firstborn among many brethren'**. 'Many' refers to all of the brethren. In Colossians 1, He is the firstborn that in all things, in both the old and the new creation, He might have pre-eminence. Here in Romans 8, among His own brethren, He has the firstborn place. Of the nine times in the New Testament the term is used, it is only in Luke 2 and Hebrews 11 that it is a time term. Outside of these references it is a term of dignity and supremacy. Thus, for instance, He is the firstborn from death.

Christ is never spoken of as our elder brother, though He calls us brethren. He stands in unique relation to the Father. In John 20 He does not say, 'our Father and our God' but 'My Father and your father, my God and your God'. 'My God' and 'your God' is not an equal relationship.

v. 30 **Moreover whom he did predestinate, them he also called: and whom he called, them he also justified: and whom he justified, them he also glorified.**

'**Moreover**' introduces the development of the subject of our eternal good. Verse 29 is from eternity to eternity but now in verse 30 the call is in time, according to purpose and consistent with God's character. It is an effectual call. In terms of offer, Rom. 4, God justifies the ungodly, but in terms of purpose the '**called**' are justified.

It is important to observe and preserve the relationship of 'whom' and 'them'. The order in the verse is sequential. There is no reference to the basis of '**justification**', His blood, or the means, faith, because the call is according to divine purpose which is God's side. Sovereignty and responsibility are not truths at variance with each other so they do not need reconciling. We do not know all God knows but by faith we accept what He has been pleased to reveal. The call of God brings eternal counsel into time.

'**Glorified**' is a broad expression. In justification I am absolved from guilt but in glorification there is the anticipation of all that lies before.

All of these are in the aorist or point tense. They have been accomplished once and for all and thus all were made good to us in eternity. The aorist introduces certainty and affords no support for a 'fall away' doctrine. This is true even for backsliders, which we all are from time to time. My reactions in time cannot undo the purpose of God. In fact, the aorist point of all five matters mentioned by the apostle is just one point. As to the conception of divine purpose we look at foreknowledge and predestination; as to its conduct we look at calling and justification; its consummation shall be when we are actually glorified. However, all of these are viewed in the divine mind as completed. Thus, in verse 31, He will freely give us all things, namely the 'all things' of divine purpose, the same 'all things' that are referred to in verse 28. These are freely given, gratuitously and without cause.

Three questions follow in the next verses in which the apostle speaks of inward fears and, from verse 35, of outward fears. In verse 31, 'What shall we say then?', in verse 33, 'What can anyone say?', and in verse 36, 'What can anyone do?'

v. 31   **What shall we then say to these things? If God be for us, who can be against us?**

Verses 31-34 bring before us a court scene: the apostle uses the words 'for' and 'against'. There is no doubt that God is for us, the evidence being that He has freely given us all things as a gift of grace. There are, of course, those who are against those who are the objects of divine blessing, but none can be ultimately successful. In view of all that the apostle has said the word '**if**' does not introduce doubt but bears the significance of 'since'.

v. 32   **He that spared not his own Son, but delivered him up for us all, how shall he not with him also freely give us all things?**

There is conclusive evidence that God is for us. '**All things**' are the five links of purpose. Here Paul reasons from the greater to the lesser. What is foreknowledge, predestination, calling, justification and glorification compared with God not sparing His Son? The use of '**how**' indicates the absolute certainty the apostle has.

This verse is often misquoted. It is not that He 'freely gave' His own Son; rather, He 'did not spare' Him but freely gives us all things. No less a person than '**his own Son**' was not withheld and was delivered up, in unrelenting justice, to the death of the cross. The apostle speaks neither of a created son, nor an adopted son but of His own eternal Son. Verse 3 also speaks of 'His own Son', though it is not quite the same expression. Verse 3 speaks of His greatness but verse 32 of His preciousness.

'**Sparing**' is Calvary, not just His sparing Him from His side. The stroke of judgement here was from the hand of One to whom He was so precious. It was God who '**delivered him up for us all**'. '**For**' is 'on behalf of' and it is not here the question of the world but of 'us'. God did not merely permit the cross but purposed it. In chapter 4 verse 25 He was 'delivered up' for our offences; the same act is in view here. Calvary is the proof that God is for us. Man delivered Him up, Matt. 27. 2; the Son of God delivered Himself up, Gal. 2. 20. God here delivers Him up sacrificially. When dealing with Christ sacrificially Scripture will always speak in terms of God, not the Father. Of the seven cries on the cross the first and last were to the Father but the central cry regarding His being forsaken was to His God. A holy God deals with Christ as man.

v. 33   **Who shall lay any thing to the charge of God's elect? It is God that justifieth.**

In this court scene those in the dock have been freely given all things; they are '**God's elect**', foreknown, predestinated, called, justified, glorified. No Christian is sinless but, in the context, the charge an accuser makes is against God's elect who are seen in the dock as the beneficiaries of God's free grace. This is to do, then, with eternal security.

An accuser arises. Revelation chapter 12 verse 10 speaks of the devil as the one who accused the brethren before God day and night. He rises to his feet in the court and accuses God's elect of guilt and sin. The accusing voice, wherever it comes from, is silenced by God Himself. '**It is God that justifieth**'. This is not a question but a statement which silences every accusing voice. Justification is complete and eternal. Acts chapter 13 verse 39 says, 'By him all that believe are justified from all things'. Full satisfaction has been made for their sins and they are justified, beyond the charge of all. This sets aside all possibility of sin being raised at the *bema*.

v. 34   **Who is he that condemneth? It is Christ that died, yea rather, that is risen again, who is even at the**

right hand of God, who also maketh intercession for us.

Laying something to one's charge has in view accusation being made. To **'condemn'** is to demand a sentence on the basis of proven guilt. The Law demanded condemnation because it has been broken. An advocate, with the marks of Calvary on His body, intercedes for them. He says, 'I am God's Son; I was not spared; my sacrifice was to secure the justification of those whose condemnation you seek. I am now alive; God is satisfied and I am at His right hand as proof of this'. Thus, He makes intercession for us and no sentence can be passed.

In verse 27 His intercession for us is in relation to unuttered petitions but here it is against a demand for our condemnation. This is not **'intercession'** in pleading but in all the acceptability of His sacrifice. Elsewhere, He is engaged in high priestly intercession also. That He is risen shows divine acceptance of His sacrifice; His presence before the face of God is our assurance that every claim has been met. Thus, the accusing voice is silenced and every claim for condemnation quashed. God is for us; He has acquitted us of guilt. Christ intercedes for us in the unquestionable acceptance of Calvary. This stills all inward fear; I am eternally secure.

It should be noted that when Scripture speaks of the death of 'Jesus' it refers to that which is historical whereas the death of 'Christ' is representative.

v. 35   **Who shall separate us from the love of Christ? shall tribulation, or distress, or persecution, or famine, or nakedness, or peril, or sword?**

From this verse to the end of the chapter the apostle speaks of outward fear, as God's people, seen as defenceless sheep, are in a hostile world. The fact that God is for us does not make us immune from forces being against us, yet none of these is able to separate us from the love of Christ. No extreme of time or space, dying or living, or the spirit world can separate us from the love of God which spared not His own Son. The 'love of God . . . in Christ Jesus our Lord' is divine love maintained undiminished in God's own Son.

The question raised relates not to being separated from Christ but from the **'love of Christ'**, as it is this that sustains us in a hostile world in which we are more than conquerors. His love which was displayed at Calvary remains undiminished and sustains us in all troubles. It will never desert us or be withdrawn from us in all the trials of life. We have a constant nearness to the love of Christ.

'**Tribulation**' is a general word and the following words particularise it. '**Distress**' has the idea of people being in dire straits with no relief. '**Persecution**' is being pursued. '**Famine**', a scarcity of food and '**nakedness**', an absence of shelter and clothing. '**Peril**', with its danger, and the '**sword**', with its violent death, are all extremes to which the people of God are exposed. However, no matter the extremity, the devil cannot gain the victory. He can kill the body but do no more.

v. 36   **As it is written, For thy sake we are killed all the day long; we are accounted as sheep for the slaughter.**

The citation is from Psalm 44 verse 22. To be in these extremes was not merely something Paul spoke about but it was a real experience for him. This enables him to say in verse 38, 'I am persuaded'.

Three things are mentioned. The occasion of suffering is that it is '**for thy sake**'. It is not our own folly in view here but rather it is for His sake. The apostle speaks of being 'delivered unto death for Jesus' sake', 2 Cor. 4. 11. That so many of us do not suffer has caused us to settle down and become worldly. The constancy of suffering is seen in that it is '**all the day long**'; there is a constant exposure to suffering. The character of the suffering is that we are '**accounted as sheep for the slaughter**'. Sheep are defenceless and continually exposed to slaughter. In Isaiah 53 He was as a sheep and we are called to tread the path He trod.

No particular person does the accounting; the apostle merely states that that is just the way it is.

v. 37   **Nay, in all these things we are more than conquerors through him that loved us.**

'**We are more than conquerors**' in the strength of that love as we come through extreme circumstances not merely with faith unimpaired but stronger. What is emphasised here, then, is being strengthened by divine love. '**Loved us**' is from the standpoint of looking back after the trial is finished; it is seen in retrospect. If faith and love remain undiminished in the trial I conquer but if these things are increased I am more than a conqueror.

vv. 38-39 **For I am persuaded, that neither death, nor life,**
nor angels, nor principalities, nor powers,
nor things present, nor things to come,
Nor height, nor depth, nor any other creature,
shall be able to separate us from the love of God,
which is in Christ Jesus our Lord.

No extreme can shut us out from the love of God. '**I am persuaded**' does not suggest that Paul had wavered and needed persuasion but that he was 'assured on good grounds'. He is persuaded as he has become more than conqueror.

If I have to pass through '**death**', I will not be separated from the love of God and '**life**', with all its problems, will not separate me from it either. '**Angels**' and '**principalities**' are unseen spiritual beings. '**Powers**' are seen and unseen, men or angels. These cannot separate me from divine love, neither can '**things present**' nor '**things to come**'. Thus, the apostle embraces in his list things around me at present and things which will come in my future days. There is no mention of 'past' here. He takes it for granted that we have learnt by experience that we will not be separated from the love of God. '**Height**' and '**depth**' speak of heaven and earth, or heaven and hell, or both. If there is any other created being which is not mentioned it is also not able to separate us from the love of God which reaches us in all its fullness through Christ Jesus our Lord.